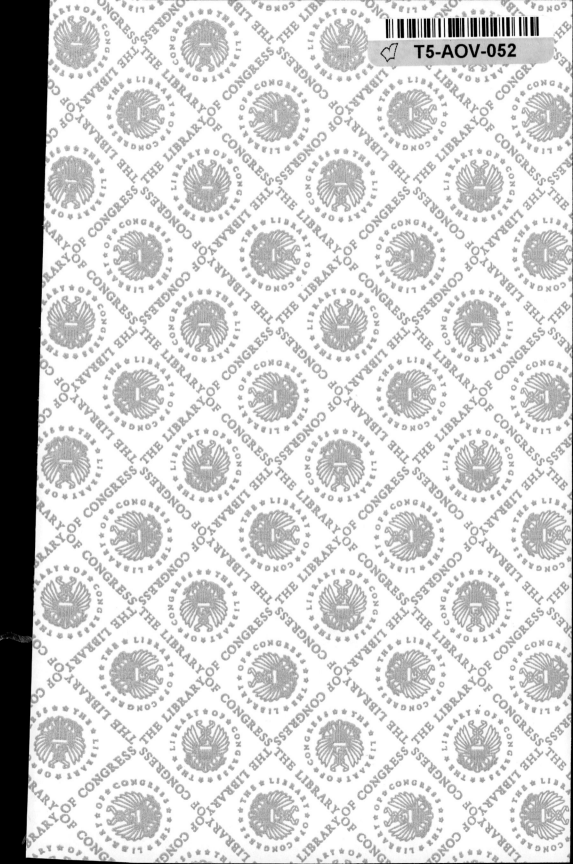

MOUNTAIN BIKE!

AMERICA
BY MOUNTAIN BIKE SERIES

New Hampshire

A GUIDE TO THE CLASSIC TRAILS

JEFF FAUST

MOUNTAIN BIKE!
New Hampshire

MOUNTAIN BIKE!
New Hampshire

A GUIDE TO THE CLASSIC TRAILS

JEFF FAUST

Menasha
Ridge
Press

Photos by the author unless otherwise credited
Maps by Steven Jones
Cover Photo by Dennis Coello

Menasha Ridge Press
700 South 28th Street
Suite 206
Birmingham, Alabama 35233

All the trails described in this book are legal for mountain bikes. But rules can change—especially for off-road bicycles, the new kid on the outdoor recreation block. Land access issues and conflicts between bicyclists, hikers, equestrians, and other users can cause the rewriting of recreation regulations on public lands, sometimes resulting in a ban of mountain bike use on specific trails. That's why it's the responsibility of each rider to check and make sure that he or she rides only on trails where mountain biking is permitted.

CAUTION

Outdoor recreational activities are by their very nature potentially hazardous. All participants in such activities must assume the responsibility for their own actions and safety. The information contained in this guidebook cannot replace sound judgment and good decision-making skills, which help reduce risk exposure, nor does the scope of this book allow for disclosure of all the potential hazards and risks involved in such activities.

Learn as much as possible about the outdoor recreational activities in which you participate, prepare for the unexpected, and be cautious. The reward will be a safer and more enjoyable experience.

To Wolfgang, who has transformed everything.

CONTENTS

LIST OF MAPS

MOUNTAIN BIKE! · Map Legend

Ride trailhead

Primary bike trail   Direction of travel   Optional bike trail and trailhead   Other trail   Hiking-only trail

Interstate highways   US routes   State routes   Other paved roads   Unpaved roads *(may be 4WD only)*

Scale   True north   Cities and towns   US Forest Service roads   State border

Public lands*   Ski Trails   Ski Lift   River or stream

✈ Airport

♥ Archeological or historical site

Boat ramp

▲ Campground (CG)

≡ Cattle guard

Cemetery or gravesite

♠ Church

Drinking water

Fire tower or lookout

Falls or rapids

Food

Gate

House or cabin

Lodging

Mountain pass

△ Mountain summit
3312 *(elevation in feet)*

Mine or quarry

Park office or ranger station

Picnic area

Power line or pipeline

Rest rooms

Spring

Stable, corral, or ranch

Swimming Area

Transmission towers

Tunnel or bridge

* *Remember, private property exists in and around our national forests.*

NEW HAMPSHIRE · Ride Locations

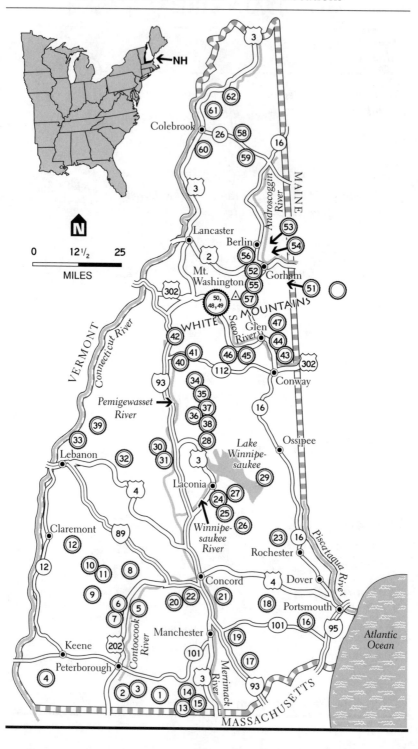

NH

MAINE

Colebrook

Lancaster

Berlin

Mt. Washington

Gorham

WHITE MOUNTAINS

VERMONT

Connecticut River

Androscoggin River

Saco River

Glen

Conway

Ossipee

Pemigewasset River

Lebanon

Lake Winnipe-saukee

Laconia

Winnipe-saukee River

Claremont

Rochester

Concord

Dover

Portsmouth

Manchester

Piscataqua River

Keene

Peterborough

Contoocook River

Merrimack River

Atlantic Ocean

MASSACHUSETTS

N

0   12½   25

MILES

ACKNOWLEDGMENTS

This book is a compilation of the knowledge, experience, opinions, and future plans of many people involved in New Hampshire's mountain biking scene. I'm just the guy who gathered up all this stuff and put it into publishable form. Without the cooperation and generosity of the shop personnel, resort managers, public officials, park rangers, and bikers-on-the-trail who know New Hampshire best, this book would not have been possible. Thanks to all who provided valuable help, including Doug Beauregard, Paul Bergeron, Andrew Boardman, Stacy Clark, Carisa Flood, Bill Fraser, Paul Giblin, John Gillen, Tim Gotwols, Paul Gray, Brian Heath, Will Hurley, Sue Liston, Patrick Manion, David Mark, Andy McBride, John McCall, James McDonough, Mike Micucci, Paul Mikalauskas, Peter Minnich, Phil Musante, Paul Otis, Nate Polzer, John Rankin, Cort Roussel, Andrea Shannon, Bob Spoerl, Chris Stevens, Eric Stinson, Donald Tase Jr., Ben Wilcox, and Cheryl Wilson, as well as the Nordic Skier in Wolfeboro and the people from the Squam Lakes Association and Hillsborough Historical Society, whose names I've somehow misplaced. Thanks also to the ladies of the Sunapee Mountain Grange, to the proprietors of the Gorham Quik-Stop, to the employees of Dunkin Donuts franchises throughout the state, to the shopping-plaza managers who ignored my little white Datsun (and the accompanying snoring) at the far ends of their lots, and to the courteous law enforcement officials who didn't.

Thanks as well to Paul Angiolillo, the author of *Mountain Biking Northern New England* and other guides. We began as coauthors and, through a rather complicated chain of events, became competitors. Paul was nonetheless most generous in supplying maps, lodging, and advice when I really needed it. Series editor Dennis Coello—the man who clarified my prose, spurred my resolve, and taught me how to remove freewheels with a Pocket Vise—gets a heapin' helping of my gratitude for his labors. Ditto for the indefatigable worker bees in the Menasha Ridge hive.

Don Olney owns a place called The Toycrafter here at home; Bruce Hawkes helps keep it running. Both have seen fit to provide steady employment to someone who runs around the shop muttering about New Hampshire, sends FedEx letters to Birmingham, Alabama on the company account, and sometimes disappears for days at a time. For this, I owe them great thanks.

Special thanks go to David Nesbitt, whose guest room, bookshelf, and Red Dwarf videos provided much-needed relief from the woods. Special thanks also to Kristen Laine and Jim Collins for, among many other kindnesses, the use of their cabin on Blueberry Island. (How much help with painting do you need *next* summer?)

Those in the habit of reading acknowledgment pages know that no author could ever possibly complete a book without the patience and understanding of his or her spouse. Now I know it from experience. During the weeks I was away on research, my wife Gail Stephens kept household affairs together, forwarded messages, and most importantly, cared for our new son. She also let me use this project as a "get out of diaper changing free" card (usually). For all this, I've promised to build more bookshelves and convert our Macintosh Plus into a talking cookbook—a lopsided bargain if ever there was one.

Lastly, thanks to Genesee Mike, the best damned steed a cyclist ever had. Another odyssey concluded, ol' hoss.

FOREWORD

Welcome to *Mountain Bike!*, a series designed to provide all-terrain bikers with the information they need to find and ride the very best trails around. Whether you're new to the sport and don't know where to pedal, or an experienced mountain biker who wants to learn the classic trails in another region, this series is for you. Drop a few bucks for the book, spend an hour with the detailed maps and route descriptions, and you're prepared for the finest in off-road cycling.

My role as editor of this series is simple: First, find a mountain biker who knows the area and loves to ride. Second, ask that person to spend a year researching the most popular and very best rides around. And third, have that rider describe each trail in terms of difficulty, scenery, condition, elevation change, and all other categories of information that are important to trail riders. "Pretend you've just completed a ride and met up with fellow mountain bikers at the trailhead," I told each author. "Imagine their questions, be clear in your answers."

As I said, the *editorial* process—that of sending out riders and reading the submitted chapters—is a snap. But the work involved in finding, riding, and writing about each trail is enormous. In some instances our authors' tasks are made easier by the information contributed by local bike shops or cycling clubs, or even by the writers of local "where-to" guides. Credit for these contributions is provided, when appropriate, in each chapter, and our sincere thanks goes to all who have helped.

But the overwhelming majority of trails are discovered and pedaled by our authors themselves, then compared with dozens of other routes to determine if they qualify as "classic"—that area's best in scenery and cycling fun. If you've ever had the experience of pioneering a route from outdated topographic maps, or entering a bike shop to request information from local riders who would much prefer to keep their favorite trails secret, or know how it is to double- and triple-check data to be positive your trail information is correct, then you have an idea of how each of our authors has labored to bring about these books. You and I, and all the mountain bikers of America, are the richer for their efforts.

You'll get more out of this book if you take a moment to read the Introduction's explanation of the trail listings. The "Topographic Maps" section will help you understand how useful topos will be on a ride, and will also tell you where to get them. And though this is a "where-to," not a "how-to," guide, those of you who have not traveled the backcountry might find "Hitting the Trail" of particular value.

In addition to the material above, newcomers to mountain biking might want to spend a minute with the Glossary, page 192, so that terms like *hardpack*, *single-track*, and *waterbars* won't throw you when you come across them in the text.

Finally, the tips in the Afterword on mountain biking etiquette and the land-use controversy might help us all enjoy the trails a little more.

All the best.

Dennis Coello
St. Louis

PREFACE

"Live Free or Die." The advertising slogan for some West Coast bike manufacturer, right? The rallying cry of a trail-access organization, perhaps? Something uttered by a downhill racer leaving the chute?

No—it's the state motto of New Hampshire. Even better, it's a reflection of the state's attitude toward mountain biking. Throughout my travels, I kept asking anyone in a position to know, "Have there been any trail-access controversies or problems?" I only found one (the full story is given in the last chapter).

Off-road bicycling dovetails perfectly with New Hampshire's heritage of outdoor recreation. Residents accept it; state and federal agencies encourage it; institutional landowners permit it; bike shops support it; a sizable tourism industry promotes it; and loggers and snowmobilers have blazed trails for it. While mountain bikers elsewhere fight for basic trail access, New Hampshire's fat-tire aficionados enjoy "open unless closed" policies on most public lands. The riding varies from easy to highly technical, from paved paths to single-track, from flat to the highest peaks in the northeastern United States. By any reckoning, the Granite State is a great place to ride.

Let's talk a little about some of the factors that make New Hampshire mountain biking what it is.

DIVISION OF PARKS AND RECREATION

The Division of Parks and Recreation is the New Hampshire state agency responsible for setting policies in state parks and on state-owned trails. Their attitude toward mountain bikes is, I'm happy to say, a very positive one. Most of their lands (they manage about 178,000 acres) are open. In some cases, they'll close a trail for environmental or safety reasons and mark it with a "no bikes" sign. So far, user conflicts, the bane of mountain bikers elsewhere, have not been a problem on their lands.

I spent an afternoon talking to Paul Gray and Bob Spoerl in the division's Trails Bureau. Besides administering state-owned recreational trails like the

Sugar River trail, they manage the state's snowmobile trail system. Every snow-mobiler in New Hampshire pays for a registration sticker. The state collects over a million bucks per season this way, and more than 80 percent of that money is distributed to snowmobile clubs around the state for trail maintenance, which is performed by an estimated 5,000 volunteers. Most of the 5,200 miles in the state's snowmobile trail system is on private land, which is made possible by the program's landowner liability coverage.

The bureau would like to see a similar program implemented for mountain bikes, and some off-roaders have expressed interest. It wouldn't be easy, of course. A lot of cyclists would grumble about having to pay to ride. Mountain bike clubs would have to beef up their membership and get them motivated to do trail work. But imagine the possibilities: greater trail access and maintenance, better signage and mapping. It's an exciting vision for the future of mountain biking.

WHITE MOUNTAIN NATIONAL FOREST

Not all national forests welcome mountain bikes like the White Mountain National Forest does. The Forest attracts a lot of cyclists, and rangers say they've observed few problems with erosion or user conflicts. You're asked to stay off the Appalachian Trail and out of the five designated wilderness areas within the park, but the rest of the place—all 763,502 acres of it—is pretty much yours. The next few years will see the development of an area specifically set aside for mountain biking, too.

There is one catch, however. In 1997 the *Passport to the White Mountain National Forest* was created—in other words, a parking sticker. It's a pilot program intended to help the park pay its way in this era of shrinking federal budgets. Forest Service literature promises that 80 percent of the money goes right back into forest maintenance and improvements. All unattended vehicles parked on land administered by the Forest Service are required to display the *Passport*. A $5 *Passport* is valid for seven consecutive days; $20 annual *Passports* are also available. Get them at Forest Service Visitor Centers or from selected retailers in nearby towns. (Rides with trailheads on national forest land are noted; alternative parking arrangements are given wherever possible.)

The White Mountain National Forest's Visitor Centers can be found in Plymouth, Conway, Bethlehem, and Gorham. The address for main headquarters is White Mountain National Forest, P.O. Box 638, Laconia, NH 03247, phone (603) 528-8721.

RESORTS

Why *pay* to ride at a resort when you can do it for free elsewhere? Resort operators like to point out that they "add value" to your riding experience. Your fee gets you a better groomed trail, blazing and signage that make sense (usually), and even an accurate map (often in full color, and usually with contours). It's mountain biking without the headaches. Often, the most difficult task is comprehending all the legalese in the lengthy waiver you'll be asked to sign.

Because it's such a young business, operators are still learning that cyclists have different needs on the trails than skiers. As mountain biking becomes a bigger draw, they're cutting better trails, altering their maintenance procedures, and upgrading their signage. And virtually every one of them is working on a better map (or so they told me). Ride the resorts for the next few years, and you're bound to see some marked improvements. (Or, ride now and avoid the long lift lines.)

Resort mountain biking, like resort skiing, comes in two varieties: cross-country and lift-serviced.

Cross-country trails are laid out over rolling terrain, and are well suited for beginning mountain bikers (or experienced ones looking for an easy ride). In most cases, the trails climb only partway up the surrounding hillsides, although some systems have trails that will take you right to the peak.

Lift-serviced facilities whisk you on a chair lift or gondola to the top of a downhill trail network. They're more expensive, and they're not for beginners. Downhilling is an exciting sport, has received loads of press coverage lately, and provides great action photos for resort brochures (or soft-drink ads, or what have you). The problem is, most cyclists lack the skills to downhill safely. Even a gentle ski run makes a pretty fast bike trail. Resort operators screen customers carefully and discourage novices. Because so many mountain bikers *are* novices, however, this isn't the easiest way to pay the bills. Expect the lift-serviced scene to remain in a state of flux while operators figure out how to make their trails appealing to a broader audience of cyclists (or give up trying).

Having a good bike is especially important in downhilling. Most resorts have high-end machines available for rental. So if your fork is too rigid or your brakes too weak, leave yours behind and ride one of theirs. (A practical note: On most lifts, your bike will ride to the top hanging by its front wheel. Make sure your accessories are secure, your bag zipped, and your water bottles closed.)

Interested in giving downhilling a try, but not quite sure if you've got what it takes? When you get your lift ticket, ask about riding down the maintenance road. It's the easiest—and longest—way down most mountains. You'll have an exciting ride without the white-knuckle experience of a steeper trail.

For this edition of the book, I was unable to evaluate two New Hampshire lift-serviced resorts: Wildcat, which was shut down pending installation of a new gondola, and Attitash, whose mountain bike program had just restarted following a change in ownership. Bear them in mind as you contemplate your downhilling activities.

PAPER COMPANIES

In northern New Hampshire, most of the wilderness is owned by paper companies. Every year, about 1.5 percent of their forests gets sawed down, loaded onto large trucks, and hauled to the mills over a vast network of dirt logging roads that cyclists crave access to. Because the logging is done in small patches throughout the woods, however, few of these roads are ever completely free of trucks. Consequently, the paper companies have been hesitant to open up access for bikes, lest one be found stuck to the radiator of a southbound Brockway.

But the paper guys aren't deaf. They too own bikes, love the outdoors, and have friends in the tourism industry. Local mountain bikers are being allowed to ride on certain inactive logging roads. Out-of-towners, of course, may ride too, but this fact isn't widely known for a couple of reasons. So far, mountain bike traffic has been very light, and the paper companies wish to keep it that way to avoid conflicts. Also, available trails vary from year to year, depending on where timber is being cut.

For now, ride with the assumption that trails and private roads on paper-company land are closed unless specifically signed "open." If you see a gate across a dirt road and there's no sign saying "Bikes Allowed," turn around and head back. Don't be a bonehead and sour landowners on mountain biking by riding where you're not wanted. Open trails aren't hard to find—*if* you ask around locally.

CLUBS

It's not that there aren't any mountain biking clubs in New Hampshire. I was given the names and addresses of several. I simply didn't see any evidence of them at ground level. In the course of my travels, no cyclist I met mentioned membership in a club; no shop counter or bulletin board I saw had membership forms; no group ride I heard of was organized by a local IMBA affiliate. (There were several NORBA competitive events around the state, though.) Group rides and advocacy activities are centered around bike shops instead.

New Hampshire does have one established bike club: the Granite State Wheelmen (GSW). Their primary focus is road cycling, but there's a lot of mountain biking going on among the membership, too. In my days as a bike-club newsletter editor, I received newsletters from other clubs all over the eastern United States. Most were little more than ride schedules and shop ads; GSW's was one of the few with real articles in it. For that alone, it might be worth your while to join. Send a self-addressed stamped envelope to the Granite State Wheelmen, 9 Veterans Road, Amherst, NH 03031 for membership information.

RAIL TRAILS

Railroads were the interstates of the nineteenth century, and back then, New Hampshire had a lot of them. Lines branched out from Concord, Portsmouth, and Nashua to cross the entire state. As paved highways and Model Ts proliferated, however, rails were gradually taken up, leaving behind miles of empty, level right-of-ways. Today, these roadbeds make for some of the easiest riding you'll find anywhere.

As abandoned right-of-ways have come up for sale in recent years, the State of New Hampshire has been working to acquire as many of them as possible, not only for trail use, but to "landbank" the corridor for possible future transportation or utility purposes. Quite a bit of mileage has been preserved this way. Only a small portion of it is ready for mountain bikers now; development of the remainder is being done as resources allow.

There's an advocacy organization devoted to developing old railroad beds for recreational use: the Rails-to-Trails Conservancy. They provide help to local trail activists and also publish a guidebook of rail trails across the nation. Write them at 1400 Sixteenth Street NW, Washington, DC 20036. A handy reference for finding old railroad beds in your area is *Right-of-Way* by the late Waldo Nielsen (Maverick Publications, 1992), with state-by-state listings for over 80,000 route-miles of abandoned railroads, including 543 route-miles in New Hampshire.

CLASS VI ROADS

Much of New Hampshire's mountain biking is done on what are known as Class VI roads. These are old, unmaintained town roads, generally suitable for Jeeps and snowmobiles. Sometimes a Class VI is an easy double-track trail. Often, the hilly portions have eroded into a barely ridable river of boulders. They are rarely marked (except sometimes with snowmobile trail blazes; Class VI roads are a key part of that system). Stone fences are a distinguishing characteristic of Class VIs. You'll see them along one or both sides, just into the trees, and know that the road dates back to the nineteenth century.

SNOWMOBILE TRAILS

Snowmobiling is a *huge* winter activity in New Hampshire, and at $365 million annually, second only to skiing in the tourism it generates. An extensive statewide trail network is maintained by local clubs using registration-fee revenue. Clubs often maintain their own local trails as well. Some of the trails make good riding in the off-season. (Because many trails cross private land, summer access is not universal; inquire locally before hitting the woods with a snowmobiler map.) They're usually blazed (most commonly with orange-plastic diamond-shaped markers, and sometimes a state route number as well), which makes them fairly easy to follow.

Snowmobilers afford local mountain bikers another opportunity: winter mountain biking. Yes, that's right, when snow and weather conditions are just right, mountain bikers get together, mount their lights, and hit those smooth, hard-packed trails. Who says you need skis to enjoy the outdoors in wintertime?

SEASONS

Early spring is mud time in the Granite State. While there are bikers who revel in the ooze, trail administrators discourage riding because of erosion concerns, and most cyclists opt to wait until things dry out. This begins to happen in late

April in the southern counties. In the North Country it may not take place until early June.

Early summer is when the bugs are thickest. Depending on the area, you'll be swatting black flies, deer flies, mosquitoes, or other winged carnivores. Repellents containing DEET reduce the problem but don't eliminate it. Riding on a cool day helps considerably.

The bugs start to fade as berry season arrives in July. Yes, even the White Mountains get hot and muggy at the height of summer, but the wilderness is sprinkled with wild blueberries and raspberries, small but tasty. A short romp through the berry patch can make up for a spell of bad riding.

The tourism season runs throughout the summer. The White Mountains and the Lakes Country fill up with vacationers, and on weekends, urban New England heads inland to beat the heat. This is the time to be most wary of trail conflicts.

Things calm down, and cool down, in September. The crowds leave, the evenings get cold, and resorts cut back on hours, but the days are warm and riding is a pleasure.

As October arrives, so do the fall colors, working their way north to south across the forests. Briefly, the tourists return, to gaze at mountains wrapped in crimson and gold. On sunny days, the riding is still good; not so on chill, rainy ones. Daylight hours become short, and hunting season begins. More and more mountain bikers start hibernating.

By November, it's just about over. Snow begins to fly, and mats of slippery wet leaves blanket the trails. All but the very boldest have hung up the bikes for the year.

In winter, however, a hardy few keep watch for an opportunity to ride. At just the right moment—when the weather is clear and the snowmobile trails packed and smooth—word gets around to local cyclists. They mount lights, don wool and Gore-tex, and get together for an off-road adventure in the snow.

MAPS

The long-awaited topographic version of DeLorme's *New Hampshire Atlas and Gazetteer* (DeLorme, Freeport, Maine 04032) came out in 1996. The DeLorme is, by and large, a pretty good reference, but marred by flaws in the fine print. Some of the roads and trails marked on the map are nonexistent ("A lot of what they've mapped was wiped out in the '38 hurricane," says one expert from Conway), and some significant features are mislocated. If you plan to spend much time in the Granite State, get one anyway. (DeLorme also has a nifty CD-ROM map of America, but the level of detail is too low to be useful for mountain biking.)

Some of the rides in this book refer to specific pages of the 1996 edition of the DeLorme Atlas, the edition current at this writing. Future editions of the atlas may not share the same pagination. In that case, look up the town mentioned as the "general location" of the ride in the index of your atlas to locate your destination.

The old standby in outdoor maps is, of course, the United States Geological Survey (USGS) 7.5 minute series of topographic sheets. Much of the state is covered by provisional maps dating from around 1987. One outdoorsperson tells me, how-ever, that the new maps are *less* accurate than the older 15 minute maps. (Blame it on modern technology—when was the last time you saw an aerial camera go moun-tain biking?) USGS topos aren't terribly portable on the bike, of course, and at $4 or more retail, the sheets required for a longer ride add up quickly. As mentioned by Dennis Coello in his series introduction, you can get a statewide map index on request from the USGS. The index also lists retailers that stock the maps (usually one or two places in most mid-size towns). Alas, I discovered that many New Hampshire retailers have since dropped them (too much hassle for too little money, they told me); ask around, though, and you'll find a place that sells the sheets you need. If you have the luxury of several months' time, order directly from the USGS—you'll save time hunting for them on your trip (not to mention the markup that most retailers tack onto the $4 base price).

A practical alternative to USGS topos for some areas of New Hampshire—especially the White Mountains—is the topographic hiking maps put out by the Appalachian Mountain Club (AMC). Look for them at camping goods stores and the AMC's Visitor Center in Pinkham Notch (on NH 16, between Jackson and Gorham).

Feeling adventurous? Interested in bushwhacking your way through trails that perhaps don't see many bikers? Stop at a snowmobile dealer and ask about obtaining a snowmobiling map. As mentioned above under "snowmobiles," however, remember that snowmobile trails are frequently on private land and may not be open during the summer months (the state snowmobile registration program provides something we cyclists can't: liability coverage for landowners). Inquire at a nearby bike shop, or ask the landowner directly.

In many areas of the state, local cyclists have compiled maps or guides of the best local riding, and I've consulted with them for rides to include in this book. Bibliographic and purchasing information is listed in appropriate chapters, so you can seek out additional riding when you get there.

Okay, you've got a map—where do you put it? I wondered the same thing, and was just about to attach the big handlebar bag off my road bike, when a mysterious package arrived from CycoActive Products of Seattle, Washington. Inside were a pair of bicycle mapholders, with a friendly letter urging me to give them a try. So I did. Their deluxe model, the BarMap OTG, stayed securely Velcroed to the handlebars for the duration of my research. On the trail, it per-formed very well, holding an 8.5' × 11' map (or a xerographic copy thereof), pencil, notecards, film-exposure table, and my heavy Silva mapping compass. There are many ways to keep a map handy on the trail, but this is the best I've seen. Look for it at your favorite bike shop or mail-order catalog, or call CycoActive at (800) 491-CYCO.

Naturally, if you're packing a detailed map, you'll want to bring along a compass, too. (Not a bad idea in any case.) The best compass in the world is useless, how-ever, if you don't know how to use it. The classic how-to book on the subject is *Be Expert with Map and Compass* by Bjorn Kjellstrom; you'll find it at any good out-door retailer. If your map doesn't make any mention of magnetic declination, a set-ting of 16° West will suffice as a rough average for the state.

THE '98 ICE STORM

As this book goes to press, New Hampshire—much of New England, in fact—is recovering from the ice storm of January 1998, the most devastating storm to hit this region in 60 years. My hometown had its ice storm back in '91, and I can tell you from personal experience that such storms wreak incredible damage upon trees and forests. Consequently, some of the trails in this book will be littered with so much deadfall as to render them unrideable—at least for a while. While loggers and snowmobilers are already clearing roads most important to them, other trails may not receive proper attention for months, or even years. If you're planning a mountain bike getaway to the Granite State, call ahead and get an update on trail conditions from a bike shop, park manager, or other local authority (you'll find numbers listed in every chapter).

As much as the ice storm represents a short-term setback, it is also a long-term opportunity: lend a hand to the restoration efforts of your favorite trail, if you can, and help hasten its reopening. Volunteers are sorely needed to clear many miles of wooded trails, and there's no better way for mountain bikers to demonstrate that they deserve to be counted among legitimate trail users. Find out what local group carries out trail maintenance in your area, sign up for the next work session, and sharpen your saw. You'll be glad you did.

AND NOW, A WORD ABOUT CELLULAR PHONES . . .

Thinking of bringing the Flip-Fone along on your next off-road ride? Before you do, ask yourself the following questions:

- Do I know where I'm going? Do I have an adequate map? Can I use a compass effectively? Do I know the shortest way to civilization if I need to bail out early and find some help?

- If I'm on the trail for longer than planned, am I ready for it? Do I have adequate water? Have I packed something to eat? Will I be warm enough if I'm still out there after dark?

- Am I prepared for possible injuries? Do I have a first-aid kit? Do I know what to do in case of a cut, fracture, snakebite, or heat exhaustion?

- Is my tool kit adequate for likely mechanical problems? Can I fix a flat? Can I untangle a chain? Am I prepared to walk out if the bike is unridable?

If you answered "yes" to *every* question above, you may pack the phone, but consider a good whistle instead. It's lighter, cheaper, and nearly as effective.

If you answered "no" to *any* of these questions, be aware that your cellular phone does little to reduce your risks in the wilderness. Sure, being able to dial 911 in the farthest corner of the White Mountains sounds like a great idea, but this ain't downtown, friend. If disaster strikes, and your call is routed to some emergency operator in Manchester or Bangor, and it takes awhile to figure out which ranger, sheriff, or search-and-rescue crew to connect you with, and you can't tell the authorities where you are because you're really not sure, and the closest they can come to pinpointing your location is a cellular tower that serves 62 square miles of dense woods, and they start searching for you but dusk is only two hours away, and you have no signaling device and your throat is too dry to shout, and meanwhile you can't get the bleeding stopped, you are out of luck. I mean *really* out of luck.

And when the battery goes dead, you're on your own again.

Enough said. Let's get to the rides. I've split them up into seven regions that correspond roughly to New Hampshire's rivers, with a few words of introduction to each section. See you on the trail.

— Jeff Faust

Family riding

1 Greenville Trail
2 Annett State Forest
5 Hillsborough River Walk
6 Fox Forest Loop
7 Franklin Pierce Loop
9 Pillsbury State Park
14 Beaver Brook
21 Bear Brook State Park
22 I-89 Bike Path
29 Russel C. Chase Bridge-Falls Path
35 Waterville Valley (Cross-Country)
42 Franconia Notch State Park
44 Whitaker Woods
51 Wild River
57 Great Glen Trails
60 Bungy Road

Level riding

1 Greenville Trail
5 Hillsborough River Walk
11 Newbury Cut
12 Sugar River Trail
16 Newfields Trail
17 Rockingham Recreational Trail
22 I-89 Bike Path
29 Russel C. Chase Bridge-Falls Path
62 Lake Francis

Mountainous Riding

25 Belknap Saddle
26 Hidden Valley
30 Plymouth Mountain
31 Bridgewater Hill
32 Orange Cove Trail
36 Sandwich Notch
37 Flat Mountain Pond
38 Ridgepole Trail
39 Reservoir Pond
45 Bartlett Experimental Forest
46 Sawyer River
47 Doublehead
50 Cherry Mountain
52 The Pipeline
54 Leadmine Ledge
56 Moose Brook State Park
59 Kelsey Notch
60 Bungy Road
61 Stewartstown Hollow

Loops

4 Pisgah State Park
5 Hillsborough River Walk
6 Fox Forest Loop
7 Franklin Pierce Loop
8 Mink Hills
9 Pillsbury State Park
13 Potanipo Hill
18 Pawtuckaway State Park
23 Blue Job Mountain
24 Liberty Hill
25 Belknap Saddle
30 Plymouth Mountain
31 Bridgewater Hill
33 Boston Lot Lake
38 Ridgepole Trail
47 Doublehead
50 Cherry Mountain
52 The Pipeline
54 Leadmine Ledge
56 Moose Brook State Park
59 Kelsey Notch
60 Bungy Road

Out-and-Backs

1 Greenville Trail
2 Annett State Forest
3 Mountain Road
11 Newbury Cut
12 Sugar River Trail
19 Massabesic Lake
22 I-89 Bike Path
26 Hidden Valley
28 Chamberlain-Reynolds Memorial Forest
29 Russel C. Chase Bridge-Falls Path
32 Orange Cove Trail

Out-and-Backs (continued)

37 Flat Mountain Pond
41 Lincoln Woods Trail
46 Sawyer River
51 Wild River

53 Cascade Falls
61 Stewartstown Hollow
62 Lake Francis

Point-to-Points

16 Newfields Trail
17 Rockingham Recreational Trail

36 Sandwich Notch
42 Franconia Notch State Park

Trail Networks

4 Pisgah State Park
14 Beaver Brook
15 Hollis Town Forest
20 Hopkinton-Everett Lake Project
21 Bear Brook State Park
27 Gunstock
35 Waterville Valley (Cross-Country)

40 Loon Mountain
44 Whitaker Woods
45 Bartlett Experimental Forest
49 Bretton Woods (Cross-Country)
55 Hayes Copp Ski Trails
57 Great Glen Trails
58 The Balsams

Lift-Serviced Downhill Riding

10 Mount Sunapee State Park
34 Waterville Valley (Lift-Serviced)
40 Loon Mountain

43 Cranmore
48 Bretton Woods (Lift-Serviced)

Bring Your Binoculars

13 Potanipo Hill
32 Orange Cove Trail
38 Ridgepole Trail
42 Franconia Notch State Park

48 Bretton Woods (Lift-Serviced)
59 Kelsey Notch
61 Stewartstown Hollow

Bring Your Nature Guide

2 Annett State Forest
6 Fox Forest Loop
13 Potanipo Hill
15 Hollis Town Forest
22 I-89 Bike Path

45 Bartlett Experimental Forest
55 Hayes Copp Ski Trails
56 Moose Brook State Park
59 Kelsey Notch

Bring Your Map and Compass

30 Plymouth Mountain
31 Bridgewater Hill
45 Bartlett Experimental Forest

INTRODUCTION

Each trail in this book begins with key information that includes length, configuration, aerobic and technical difficulty, trail conditions, scenery, and special comments. Additional description is contained in 11 individual categories. The following will help you to understand all of the information provided.

Trail name: Trail names are as designated on United States Geological Survey (USGS) or Forest Service or other maps, and/or by local custom.

At a Glance Information

Length/configuration: The overall length of a trail is described in miles, unless stated otherwise. The configuration is a description of the shape of each trail—whether the trail is a loop, out-and-back (that is, along the same route), figure eight, trapezoid, isosceles triangle, decahedron . . . (just kidding), or if it connects with another trail described in the book. See the Glossary for definitions of *point-to-point* and *combination*.

Aerobic difficulty: This provides a description of the degree of physical exertion required to complete the ride.

Technical difficulty: This provides a description of the technical skill required to pedal a ride. Trails are often described here in terms of being paved, unpaved, sandy, hard-packed, washboarded, two- or four-wheel-drive, single-track or double-track. All terms that might be unfamiliar to the first-time mountain biker are defined in the Glossary.

   Note: For both the aerobic and technial difficulty categories, authors were asked to keep in mind the fact that all riders are not equal, and thus to gauge the trail in terms of how the middle-of-the-road rider—someone between the newcomer and Ned Overend—could handle the route. Comments about the trail's length, condition, and elevation change will also assist you in determining the difficulty of any trail relative to your own abilities.

Scenery: Here you will find a general description of the natural surroundings during the seasons most riders pedal the trail, and a suggestion of what is to be found at special times (like great fall foliage or cactus in bloom).

Special comments: Unique elements of the ride are mentioned.

Category Information

General location: This category describes where the trail is located in reference to a nearby town or other landmark.

Elevation change: Unless stated otherwise, the figure provided is the total gain and loss of elevation along the trail. In regions where the elevation variation is not extreme, the route is simply described as flat, rolling, or possessing short steep climbs or descents.

Season: This is the best time of year to pedal the route, taking into account trail conditions (for example, when it will not be muddy), riding comfort (when the weather is too hot, cold, or wet), and local hunting seasons.

Note: Because the exact opening and closing dates of deer, elk, moose, and antelope seasons often change from year to year, riders should check with the local fish and game department or call a sporting goods store (or any place that sells hunting licenses) in a nearby town before heading out. Wear bright clothes in fall, and don't wear suede jackets while in the saddle. Hunter's-orange tape on the helmet is also a good idea.

Services: This category is of primary importance in guides for paved-road tourers, but is far less crucial to most mountain bike trail descriptions because there are usually no services whatsoever to be found. Authors have noted when water is available on desert or long mountain routes and have listed the availability of food, lodging, campgrounds, and bike shops. If all these services are present, you will find only the words "All services available in . . ."

Hazards: Special hazards like steep cliffs, great amounts of deadfall, or barbed-wire fences very close to the trail are noted here.

Rescue index: Determining how far one is from help on any particular trail can be difficult due to the backcountry nature of most mountain bike rides. Authors therefore state the proximity of homes or Forest Service outposts, nearby roads where one might hitch a ride, or the likelihood of other bikers being encountered on the trail. Phone numbers of local sheriff departments or hospitals are hardly ever provided because phones are usually not available. If you are able to reach a phone, the local operator will connect you with emergency services.

Land status: This category provides information regarding whether the trail crosses land operated by the Forest Service; Bureau of Land Management; a city, state, or national park; whether it crosses private land whose owner (at the time the author did the research) has allowed mountain bikers right of passage; and so on.

Note: Authors have been extremely careful to offer only those routes that are open to bikers and are legal to ride. However, because land ownership changes over time, and because the land-use controversy created by mountain bikes still has not completely subsided, it is the duty of each cyclist to look for and to heed signs warning against trail use. Don't expect this book to get you off the hook when you're facing some small-town judge for pedaling past a Biking Prohibited sign erected the day before you arrived. Look for these signs, read them, and heed the advice. And remember there's always another trail.

Maps: The maps in this book have been produced with great care and, in conjunction with the trail-following suggestions, will help you stay on course. But as every experienced mountain biker knows, things can get tricky in the backcountry. It is therefore strongly suggested that you avail yourself of the detailed information found in the 7.5 minute series USGS (United States Geological Survey) topographic maps. In some cases, authors have found that specific Forest Service or other maps may be more useful than the USGS quads and tell how to obtain them.

Finding the trail: Detailed information on how to reach the trailhead and where to park your car is provided here.

Sources of additional information: Here you will find the address and/or phone number of a bike shop, governmental agency, or other source from which trail information can be obtained.

Notes on the trail: This is where you are guided carefully through any portions of the trail that are particularly difficult to follow. The author also may add information about the route that does not fit easily in the other categories. This category will not be present for those rides where the route is easy to follow.

ABBREVIATIONS

The following road-designation abbreviations are used in the *Mountain Bike!* series:

CR	County Road	I-	Interstate
FR	Farm Route	IR	Indian Route
FS	Forest Service road	US	United States highway

State highways are designated with the appropriate two-letter state abbreviation, followed by the road number. Example: NH 417 = New Hampshire State Highway 417.

Postal Service two-letter state codes:

AL	Alabama	MT	Montana
AK	Alaska	NE	Nebraska
AZ	Arizona	NV	Nevada
AR	Arkansas	NH	New Hampshire
CA	California	NJ	New Jersey
CO	Colorado	NM	New Mexico
CT	Connecticut	NY	New York
DE	Delaware	NC	North Carolina
DC	District of Columbia	ND	North Dakota
FL	Florida	OH	Ohio
GA	Georgia	OK	Oklahoma
HI	Hawaii	OR	Oregon
ID	Idaho	PA	Pennsylvania
IL	Illinois	RI	Rhode Island
IN	Indiana	SC	South Carolina
IA	Iowa	SD	South Dakota
KS	Kansas	TN	Tennessee
KY	Kentucky	TX	Texas
LA	Louisiana	UT	Utah
ME	Maine	VT	Vermont
MD	Maryland	VA	Virginia
MA	Massachusetts	WA	Washington
MI	Michigan	WV	West Virginia
MN	Minnesota	WI	Wisconsin
MS	Mississippi	WY	Wyoming
MO	Missouri		

TOPOGRAPHIC MAPS

The maps in this book, when used in conjunction with the route directions present in each chapter, will in most instances be sufficient to get you to the trail and keep you on it. However, you will find superior detail and valuable information in the 7.5 minute series USGS topographic maps. Recognizing how indispensable these are to bikers and hikers alike, many bike shops and sporting goods stores now carry topos of the local area.

But if you're brand new to mountain biking you might be wondering, "What's a topographic map?" In short, these differ from standard "flat" maps in that they indicate not only linear distance but elevation as well. One glance at a topo will show you the difference, for "contour lines" are spread across the map like dozens of intricate spider webs. Each contour line represents a particular elevation, and at the base of each topo a particular "contour interval" designation is given. Yes, it sounds confusing if you're new to the lingo, but it truly is a simple and wonderfully helpful system. Keep reading.

Let's assume that the 7.5 minute series topo before us says "Contour Interval 40 feet," that the short trail we'll be pedaling is two inches in length on the map, and that it crosses five contour lines from its beginning to end. What do we know? Well, because the linear scale of this series is 2,000 feet to the inch (roughly 2¾ inches representing 1 mile), we know our trail is approximately ⅘ of a mile long (2 inches × 2,000 feet). But we also know we'll be climbing or descending 200 vertical feet (5 contour lines × 40 feet each) over that distance. And the elevation designations written on occasional contour lines will tell us if we're heading up or down.

The authors of this series warn their readers of upcoming terrain, but only a detailed topo gives you the information you need to pinpoint your position exactly on a map, steer yourself toward optional trails and roads nearby, plus let you know at a glance if you'll be pedaling hard to take them. It's a lot of information for a very low cost. In fact, the only drawback with topos is their size — several feet square. I've tried rolling them into tubes, folding them carefully, even cutting them into blocks and photocopying the pieces. Any of these systems is a pain, but no matter how you pack the maps, you'll be happy they're along. And you'll be even happier if you pack a compass as well.

In addition to local bike shops and sporting goods stores, you'll find topos at major universities and some public libraries where you might try photocopying the ones you need to avoid the cost of buying them. But if you want your own and can't find them locally, write to:

USGS Map Sales
Box 25286
Denver, CO 80225

Ask for an index while you're at it, plus a price list and a copy of the booklet *Topographic Maps*. In minutes you'll be reading them like a pro.

A second excellent series of maps available to mountain bikers is put out by the United States Forest Service. If your trail runs through an area designated as a national forest, look in the phone book (white pages) under the United States Government listings, find the Department of Agriculture heading, and then run your finger down that section until you find the Forest Service. Give them a call, and they'll provide the address of the regional Forest Service office, from which you can obtain the appropriate map.

TRAIL ETIQUETTE

Pick up almost any mountain bike magazine these days and you'll find articles and letters to the editor about trail conflict. For example, you'll find hikers' tales of being blindsided by speeding mountain bikers, complaints from mountain bikers about being blamed for trail damage that was really caused by horse or cattle traffic, and cries from bikers about those "kamikaze" riders who through their antics threaten to close even more trails to all of us.

The authors of this series have been very careful to guide you to only those trails that are open to mountain biking (or at least were open at the time of their research), and without exception have warned of the damage done to our sport through injudicious riding. My personal views on this matter appear in the Afterword, but all of us can benefit from glancing over the following International Mountain Bicycling Association (IMBA) Rules of the Trail before saddling up.

1. *Ride on open trails only.* Respect trail and road closures (ask if not sure), avoid possible trespass on private land, obtain permits and authorization as may be required. Federal and state wilderness areas are closed to cycling.

2. *Leave no trace.* Be sensitive to the dirt beneath you. Even on open trails, you should not ride under conditions where you will leave evidence of your passing, such as on certain soils shortly after rain. Observe the different types of soils and trail construction; practice low-impact cycling. This also means staying on the trail and not creating any new ones. Be sure to pack out at least as much as you pack in.

3. *Control your bicycle!* Inattention for even a second can cause disaster. Excessive speed can maim and threaten people; there is no excuse for it!

4. *Always yield the trail.* Make known your approach well in advance. A friendly greeting (or a bell) is considerate and works well; startling someone may cause loss of trail access. Show your respect when passing others by slowing to a walk or even stopping. Anticipate that other trail users may be around corners or in blind spots.

5. *Never spook animals.* All animals are startled by an unannounced approach, a sudden movement, or a loud noise. This can be dangerous for you, for others, and for the animals. Give animals extra room and time to adjust to you. In passing, use special care and follow the directions of horseback riders (ask if uncertain). Running cattle and disturbing wild animals is a serious offense. Leave gates as you found them, or as marked.

6. *Plan ahead.* Know your equipment, your ability, and the area in which you are riding—and prepare accordingly. Be self-sufficient at all times. Wear a helmet, keep your machine in good condition, and carry necessary supplies for changes in weather or other conditions. A well-executed trip is a satisfaction to you and not a burden or offense to others.

For more information, contact IMBA, P.O. Box 412043, Los Angeles, CA 90041, (818) 792-8830.

HITTING THE TRAIL

Once again, because this is a "where-to," not a "how-to," guide, the following will be brief. If you're a veteran trail rider, these suggestions might serve to remind you of something you've forgotten to pack. If you're a newcomer, they might convince you to think twice before hitting the backcountry unprepared.

Water: I've heard the questions dozens of times. "How much is enough? One bottle? Two? Three?! But think of all that extra weight!" Well, one simple physiological fact should convince you to err on the side of excess when it comes to deciding how much water to pack: a human working hard in 90° temperature needs approximately ten quarts of fluids every day. Ten quarts. That's two and a half gallons—12 large water bottles, or 16 small ones. And, with water weighing in at approximately eight pounds per gallon, a one-day supply comes to a whopping 20 pounds.

In other words, pack along two or three bottles even for short rides. And make sure you can purify the water found along the trail on longer routes. When writing of those routes where this could be of critical importance, each author has provided information on where water can be found near the trail—if it can be found at all. But drink it untreated and you run the risk of disease. (See *Giardia* in the Glossary.)

One sure way to kill the protozoa, bacteria, and viruses in water is to boil it. Right. That's just how you want to spend your time on a bike ride. Besides, who wants to carry a stove, or denude the countryside stoking bonfires to boil water?

Luckily, there is a better way. Many riders pack along the inexpensive and only slightly distasteful tetraglycine hydroperiodide tablets (sold under the names Potable Aqua, Globaline, and Coughlan's, among others). Some invest in portable, lightweight purifiers that filter out the crud. Unfortunately, both iodine *and* filtering are now required to be absolutely sure you've killed all the nasties you can't see. Tablets or iodine drops by themselves will knock off the well-known *giardia*, once called "beaver fever" for its transmission to the water through the feces of infected beavers. One to four weeks after ingestion, giardia will have you bloated, vomiting, shivering with chills, and living in the bathroom. (Though you won't care while you're suffering, beavers are getting a bum rap, for other animals are carriers also.)

But now there's another parasite we must worry about—*cryptosporidium*. "Crypto" brings on symptoms very similar to giardia, but unlike that fellow protozoan it's equipped with a shell sufficiently strong to protect it against the chemical killers that stop giardia cold. This means we're either back to boiling or on to using a water filter to screen out both giardia and crypto, plus the iodine to knock off viruses. All of which sounds like a time-consuming pain, but really isn't. Some water filters come equipped with an iodine chamber, to guarantee full protection. Or you can simply add a pill or drops to the water you've just filtered (if you aren't allergic to iodine, of course). The pleasures of backcountry biking—and the displeasure of getting sick—make this relatively minor effort worth every one of the few minutes involved.

Tools: Ever since my first cross-country tour in 1965 I've been kidded about the number of tools I pack on the trail. And so I will exit entirely from this discussion by providing a list compiled by two mechanic (and mountain biker) friends of mine. After all, since they make their livings fixing bikes, and get their kicks by riding them, who could be a better source?

These two suggest the following as an absolute minimum:

tire levers
spare tube and patch kit
air pump
Allen wrenches (3, 4, 5, and 6 mm)
six-inch crescent (adjustable-end) wrench
small flat-blade screwdriver
chain rivet tool
spoke wrench

But, while they're on the trail, their personal tool pouches contain these additional items:

channel locks (small)
air gauge
tire valve cap (the metal kind, with a valve-stem remover)
baling wire (ten or so inches, for temporary repairs)
duct tape (small roll for temporary repairs or tire boot)
boot material (small piece of old tire or a large tube patch)
spare chain link
rear derailleur pulley
spare nuts and bolts
paper towel and tube of waterless hand cleaner

First-Aid Kit: My personal kit contains the following, sealed inside double Ziploc bags:

sunscreen
aspirin
butterfly-closure bandages
Band-Aids
gauze compress pads (a half-dozen 4' × 4')
gauze (one roll)
ace bandages or Spenco joint wraps
Benadryl (an antihistamine, in case of allergic reactions)
water purification tablets/water filter (on long rides)
Moleskin/Spenco "Second Skin"
hydrogen peroxide, iodine, or Mercurochrome (some kind of antiseptic)
snakebite kit

Final Considerations: The authors of this series have done a good job in suggesting that specific items be packed for certain trails—raingear in particular seasons, a hat and gloves for mountain passes, or shades for desert jaunts. Heed their warnings, and think ahead. Good luck.

Dennis Coello

CONTOOCOOK
(SOUTHWESTERN NEW HAMPSHIRE)

This region is New Hampshire's art studio, the retreat district for those looking to get away—but not too far away—from the hectic pace of the Washington, DC–Boston megalopolis. Renowned American sculptor Augustus Saint-Gaudens made his summer home near Cornish, which later became his year-round residence, and ultimately the nucleus of an arts community. Another arts community arose when the widow of Edward MacDowell founded a retreat for writers near Peterborough. One MacDowell Colony resident, Thornton Wilder, set a play named *Our Town* in Grover's Corners, a fictitious town bearing a remarkable resemblance to the real Peterborough.

You'll find the New England of your imagination in this region. To describe the rolling, green hills, the white-clapboard churches, the tidy Main Streets and town squares, pick your favorite adjective: *quaint, charming, picturesque.* The beauty doesn't happen by accident; townspeople are ever vigilant against the intrusions of modern America. I witnessed one town's battle to keep a major drugstore chain from opening a new store in their village. Residents turned out in numbers at zoning-board hearings, rallying against the proposed new plaza as though it were a nuclear waste dump. One couple I met were completing an exacting restoration of a 200-year-old farmhouse. They installed electricity, reluctantly. Rather than mar the side of their home with a utility meter, they paid extra to bury the cable. (Not coincidentally, some of the best antiquing around can be had in this area, too. I came home with a vintage Coleman lantern and a few other choice bargains.)

The small mills that dotted the region were a source of great pride. Witness this entry for Claremont in the 1927 edition of AAA's *Northeastern Tour Book,* quoted here in its entirety: "The pattern paper used by the Butterick Company comes from here, and the chances are that on your next railway or steamship trip you will sleep beneath a Monadnock Spread, a product of the Monadnock mills." In fact, I spent much of my trip sleeping beneath a wool plaid blanket manufactured in nearby Guild. (In the case of the factory where Ruger firearms are made, however, pride gives way to security concerns: the sign on the building is that of a nondescript casting firm.)

The mountain biking around here tends to be over rolling terrain, in small parks and forests. The landscape is also liberally equipped with Class VI town roads (which are unmaintained dirt roads, great for riding), as well as smoother dirt roads.

Suggested Reading: Any collection of Robert Frost's poetry. Frost lived all over New England, but he's most closely identified with rural New Hampshire. His work speaks to many aspects of the New Hampshire experience and includes such classics as "Stopping by Woods on a Snowy Evening."

RIDE 1 · Greenville Trail

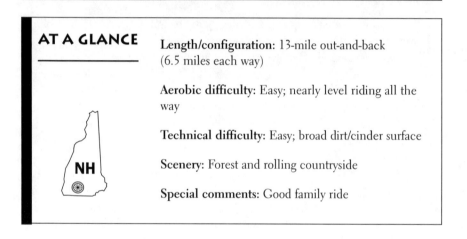

AT A GLANCE

Length/configuration: 13-mile out-and-back (6.5 miles each way)

Aerobic difficulty: Easy; nearly level riding all the way

Technical difficulty: Easy; broad dirt/cinder surface

Scenery: Forest and rolling countryside

Special comments: Good family ride

The Boston & Maine Railroad once blanketed New Hampshire with a web of branchlines. From the middle of the nineteenth century until around the 1930s or so, most of New Hampshire's travelers and freight rolled on a network of rails that fanned out from Boston and Concord. With the rise of the semi-trailer, however, most of the rails were taken up, leaving behind miles of empty railroad bed, including this one that stretches from Greenville to the Massachusetts state line.

Because of a missing bridge just north of town, you can't ride the trail right out of Greenville, but beyond that, the riding is uninterrupted to the state line.

General location: Near Greenville and Mason

Elevation change: Negligible

Season: Late spring through fall

Services: Water, food, and lodging can be found in Greenville.

Hazards: All-terrain vehicles (ATVs) aren't supposed to be on this trail, but occasionally they are, so keep an eye out for them. Use caution at road crossings.

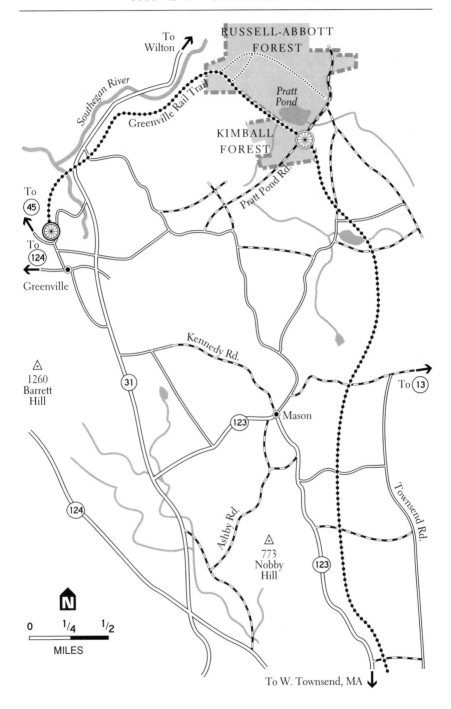

To
Wilton

RUSSELL-ABBOTT
FOREST

Southegan River

Greenville Rail Trail

Pratt
Pond

KIMBALL
FOREST

Pratt Pond Rd.

To
45

To
124

Greenville

Kennedy Rd.

1260
Barrett
Hill

31

To 13

123 Mason

124

Ashby Rd.

773
Nobby
Hill

123

Townsend Rd.

N

0   1/4   1/2
MILES

To W. Townsend, MA

Once part of a web of branchlines, now part of a growing network of trails.

Rescue index: You will be within a mile of traveled roads at all times.

Land status: State-owned railroad bed

Maps: The railroad bed is marked on page 21 of DeLorme's *New Hampshire Atlas and Gazetteer.*

Finding the trail: Watch for the remains of the old railroad bridge over NH 31 about 0.7 mile north of Greenville. Turn right onto Adams Hill Road. A small parking area is a few hundred feet beyond on the right; the trail begins to the left.

Source of additional information:

New Hampshire Division of Parks and Recreation, Trails Bureau
P.O. Box 1856
172 Pembroke Road
Concord, NH 03302-1856
(603) 271-3254

Notes on the trail: The railroad bed takes a northeasterly course to the Russell-Abbott State Forest, crosses Pratt Pond, and swings south to the state line. (The Massachusetts portion of this line, unfortunately, still has rails and ties in place.)

RIDE 2 · Annett State Forest

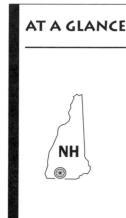

AT A GLANCE

Length/configuration: 3-mile out-and-back (1.5 miles each way)

Aerobic difficulty: Modestly undulating terrain; no prolonged climbs

Technical difficulty: Good four-wheel-drive roads with some bumpy spots

Scenery: Hardwood and pine forest

Special comments: Good family ride; Cathedral of the Pines is nearby.

NH

Tucked away on a back road between Rindge and Jaffrey, Annett State Forest is a delightful patch of quiet woods laced with dirt roads, snowmobile trails, and ponds (not to mention some of the most interesting trash I've seen dumped on New Hampshire land). You could spend the better part of a day exploring the trails, but if you prefer, this three-mile out-and-back ride will take you to the east shore of Hubbard Pond. You'll get back to the car with plenty of time to spare for a visit to the Cathedral of the Pines, just down the road.

The cathedral was built as an outdoor memorial to a son lost over Germany during World War II. Several monuments and shrines are located on the site, including the Memorial Bell Tower, which features bas-relief sculptures designed by Norman Rockwell honoring American women who helped the war effort. The cathedral is nondenominational, and free guided tours are available.

General location: South of Jaffrey

Elevation change: Park lands are gently undulating, no hard climbs here.

Season: Late spring through fall

Services: Services can be found in both Rindge (to the south) and Jaffrey (to the north).

Hazards: Watch for a few rocks in the road.

Rescue index: The forest has populated areas on all sides; civilization is never very far off.

Land status: State forest

Maps: Page 20 of DeLorme's *New Hampshire Atlas and Gazetteer*. Also see Peterborough South quadrangle, USGS 7.5 minute series.

Finding the trail: From Jaffrey (at the junction of US 202 and NH 119), take NH 119 east for 2 miles. Turn right onto Cathedral Road and follow it for about 1.2 miles, then turn left into the entrance to Annett State Forest.

RIDE 2 · Annett State Forest

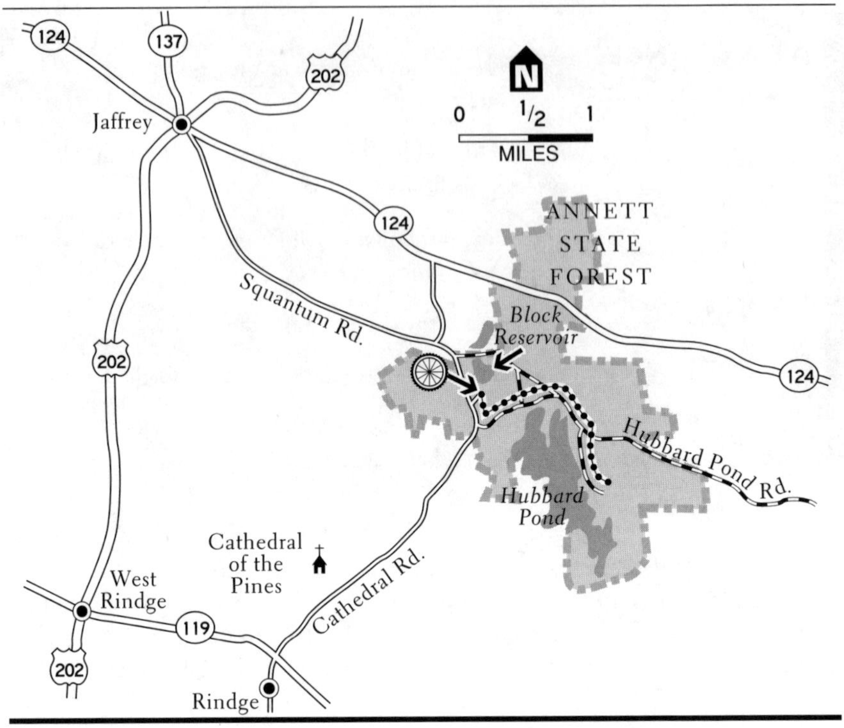

Sources of additional information:

New Hampshire Division of Forests and Lands
P.O. Box 1856
172 Pembroke Road
Concord, NH 03302-1856
(603) 271-3456

Cathedral of the Pines
75 Cathedral Entrance
Rindge, NH 03461
(603) 899-3300

Notes on the trail: Cross the field by the bus-parking area to a snowmobile trail. A short ride through the woods, parallel to the highway, brings you to a dirt road. Ride this for about 0.8 mile; it ends at Hubbard Pond Road, which is graded dirt. Bear right, watch for the pond outlet (corrugated pipes under the road), and make the first right turn afterward to the pond overlook.

Along the way, you will see additional trails, none of them marked, all of them pleasant riding. If you feel confident in your sense of direction (or your compass), explore them as the fancy strikes you.

RIDE 3 · Mountain Road

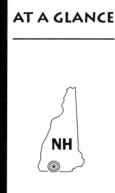

AT A GLANCE

Length/configuration: 5.5-mile out-and-back (2.8 miles each way)

Aerobic difficulty: A half mile of climbing in each direction

Technical difficulty: Heavy erosion on the northern half will challenge you.

Scenery: Rustic, wooded mountainside

Special comments: Stop by the Sharon Arts Center after the ride for arts, crafts, and live music during the summer.

This out-and-back ride follows a Class VI road through a couple of small forests and along the side of Temple Mountain, getting progressively more rugged as you head north. After cranking partway up the mountain and back down again, you emerge at Cunningham Pond on NH 101, just west of Peterborough. If you're feeling adventurous, explore the side trails on the trip back.

General location: Southeast of Peterborough on NH 123

Elevation change: About 400 feet of elevation gain in each direction

Season: Late spring through fall

Services: All services can be found in Peterborough, about 5 miles from the trailhead.

Hazards: Watch for rocks and ruts on the northern part of the trail.

Rescue index: Assistance is about a mile away at the farthest point.

Land status: Public road

Maps: Page 20 of DeLorme's *New Hampshire Atlas and Gazetteer*. Also see Greenville quadrangle, USGS 7.5 minute series.

Finding the trail: The road begins across from the Sharon Arts Center on NH 123, about 3.6 miles south of the junction with NH 101. There is a parking lot next to the trailhead; don't use the lot on the Arts Center side of the highway.

Source of additional information:

Spokes and Slopes
7 School Street
Peterborough, NH 03458
(603) 924-9961

RIDE 3 · Mountain Road

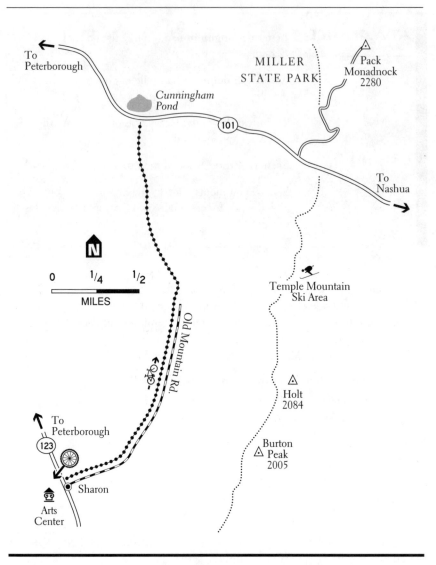

Notes on the trail: Mountain Road starts across from the Arts Center and is a graded dirt road for the first 1.5 miles. It then becomes a Class VI town road, climbs steeply for a half mile, and descends for another half mile to a clearing. Stay between the fences for the final segment to NH 101.

Just a lonely road over Temple Mountain.

RIDE 4 · Pisgah State Park

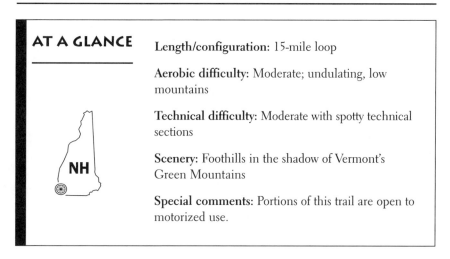

AT A GLANCE

Length/configuration: 15-mile loop

Aerobic difficulty: Moderate; undulating, low mountains

Technical difficulty: Moderate with spotty technical sections

Scenery: Foothills in the shadow of Vermont's Green Mountains

Special comments: Portions of this trail are open to motorized use.

L ocated in the southwestern corner of the state, Pisgah State Park is one of the largest parks in the state system and is mostly undeveloped. The park is liberally sprinkled with old roads and trails of varying quality; most (though not all) are open to bikes. If you're in Cheshire County and looking for a wilderness experience, this is the place to start.

This ride mostly follows old four-wheel-drive roads, with a bit of riding on narrower trails and graded dirt roads. Some of the roads along the way are open to ATV traffic, which is usually light. (User conflicts have not been a problem.)

This just in: In nearby Keene, folks have been awfully busy lately opening up rail-trail conversions and paved multiuse paths—just the ticket for family cycling. In any rail-trail construction, bridges are always the sticky part, and they've redecked over a dozen of them in 1997, with more on the way. Sounds like great stuff. Unfortunately, I heard the news too late to get the details in these pages, but you can get the full scoop from John Summers at Summers Backcountry Sports (see below).

General location: West of Keene

Elevation change: About 800 feet of climbing over the course of this ride

Season: Late spring through fall. (Bicycling is prohibited before May 23 due to muddy conditions.)

Services: All services can be found along NH 9 between the park and Keene, 8 miles to the east.

Hazards: Watch and listen for approaching ATVs and motorcycles, as well as hikers. Be prepared for changes in trail conditions.

Rescue index: Assistance will be up to 3 miles away.

Land status: State park. Please avoid trails signed "Bikes Prohibited."

Maps: Winchester quadrangle, USGS 7.5 minute series. A brochure with small maps of this and five other multiuse trails is available from the New Hampshire Division of Parks and Recreation, Bureau of Trails.

Finding the trail: From NH 9, turn south onto NH 63 and travel a mile to Chesterfield. Turn left onto Old Chesterfield Road (follow the brown signs for Pisgah State Park), proceed for about a quarter of a mile, then turn right onto Horseshoe Road, which will take you to the parking area.

Sources of additional information:

Pisgah State Park
P.O. Box 242
Winchester, NH 03470
(603) 239-8153

Friends of Pisgah
P.O. Box 1179
Keene, NH 03431

Summers Backcountry Sports
16 Ashuelot Street
Keene, NH 03431
(603) 357-5107
Proprietor John Summers also chairs the Friends of Pisgah Rails-to-Trails Committee.

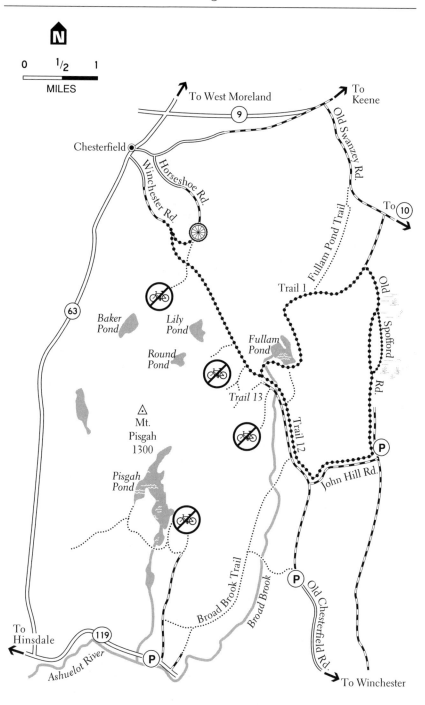

N

0   1/2   1
MILES

To West Moreland

To Keene

9

Chesterfield

Old Swanzey Rd.

Horseshoe Rd.

Winchester Rd.

To 10

Fullam Pond Trail

Trail 1

63

Baker Pond

Lily Pond

Round Pond

Fullam Pond

Old Spofford Rd.

Trail 13

Mt. Pisgah 1300

Trail 12

P

Pisgah Pond

John Hill Rd.

Broad Brook Trail

Broad Brook

P

Old Chesterfield Rd.

To Hinsdale

119

P

Ashuelot River

To Winchester

Banagan's Cycling Company
41 Central Square
Keene, NH 03431
(603) 357-2331

New Hampshire Division of Parks and Recreation, Trails Bureau
P.O. Box 1856
172 Pembroke Road
Concord, NH 03302-1856
(603) 271-3254

Notes on the trail: From the parking area, take the double-track trail downhill and bear left at the fork. You'll pass a beaver pond on your right.

After about 2.5 miles (just beyond Fullam Pond), bear right onto Old Chesterfield Road, a graded dirt road. A mile beyond, you'll see a trail junction marked "4"; this is the Broad Brook Trail to Pisgah Pond. Stay straight, and a half mile beyond, turn left onto the old asphalt road (Johns Hill Road). About a mile later, make a left onto a grassy trail, which will take you to a parking area on the park's east side. From there, turn right, then make an immediate left onto Old Spofford Road.

After a mile, bear right at the fork and travel downhill. When you get to the **T** intersection, turn left, go through the gate, and take this unmaintained road uphill. At the junction with Trail 1, bear left. Turn right at the next junction to reach Fullam Pond. Ride around the southern shore of the pond and take the bridge over the spillway. The next junction is the same one you rode through early in this ride. Turn right, and retrace your trail to the parking area.

RIDE 5 · Hillsborough River Walk

AT A GLANCE

Length/configuration: 1-mile loop

Aerobic difficulty: A short, level ride

Technical difficulty: Some mild roots, rocks, and embankments await your conquering.

Scenery: Wooded riverbank at the edge of town

Special comments: This is a good family ride; it is also a good warm-up for longer rides.

NH

In some New Hampshire town names, an "-ugh" is a matter of contention. Witness Hillsborough. Not long ago, it was known as Hillsboro, a streamlined spelling that, like *donut* or *thruway*, expressed its proper pronunciation with a minimum number of letters. This modernization of its original name took place sometime in the late nineteenth century. Hillsborough's traditional spelling is now back in fashion again (although the United States Geological Survey hasn't yet caught up).

The River Walk, tucked between Grimes Field and the river at the edge of the village, is sort of like the "modern" spelling of the town name: short, easy, and quick. It's just the thing to get the blood pumping—and make sure the derailleurs are working—before you stray too far from the car. When you and your mountain bike happen to be in town, use it as a warm-up in preparation for a day in Fox Forest. (It's good, too, for weaning young mountain bikers from asphalt to single-track.)

General location: Village of Hillsborough

Elevation change: Negligible; the trail parallels a riverbank.

Season: Spring through fall

Services: Water, food, and lodging are in town.

Hazards: Some modest surface hazards, like roots and rocks, are present. Here's a good opportunity for budding mountain bikers to start working on bike-handling skills. Watch for hikers, too.

Rescue index: Civilization is always within shouting distance.

Land status: Village park

Maps: None available, or necessary

Finding the trail: Park at Grimes Field on Preston Street and pedal around to the far side on the dirt road. Watch for the trailhead on your right.

RIDE 5 · Hillsborough River Walk

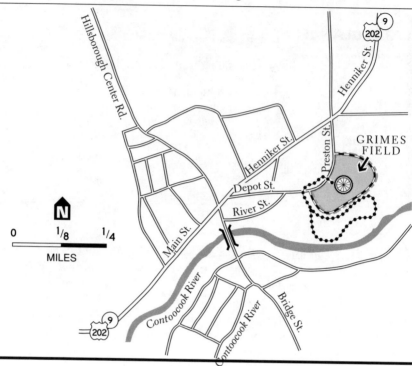

Source of additional information:

Banagan's Cycling Company
27 South Main Street
Concord, NH 03301
(603) 225-3330
Employee James McDonough (whoops—almost dropped the "-ugh")
is an authority on Hillsborough-area mountain bike riding.

Notes on the trail: The trail never strays very far from the riverbank, so the navigation is easy. You'll have fun negotiating passages between closely spaced trees and knee-high embankments. At the end, take the dirt road back to your starting point, or do a few laps around the field.

RIDE 6 · Fox Forest Loop

Length/configuration: 13-mile loop

Aerobic difficulty: Easy; some moderate climbing

Technical difficulty: Fairly easy woods trails, dirt roads, and pavement; one moderately challenging rocky descent

Scenery: Woods and rolling countryside

Special comments: Good ride for families with older children. More good riding can be found on additional trails throughout Fox Forest. Don't miss Kemp's Mack Museum on River Street!

Don't get me wrong—this is a great ride, recommended to me by the legendary Ped'ling Fool of Hillsborough himself. It takes you on a wonderful woods trail through Fox Forest, some nice town roads (both paved and dirt), and a portion of the old Contoocook Valley Railroad bed. But what I liked best were the trucks: old trucks, lots of them, of every nameplate (White, Autocar, Oshkosh, Brockway) and body style (tanker, tow truck, snowplow, furniture van), parked three-deep on River Street. Other New England towns may consider Kemp's Mack Museum an eyesore, but not Hillsborough—the museum is proudly featured in the tourist brochure. So look around, sign the guest register, and—oh yeah—don't forget to ride.

General location: Hillsborough

Elevation change: Prepare for a few hundred feet of climbing (much of it on pavement) in the first half of the ride.

Season: Late spring through fall

Services: Water, food, and lodging are in Hillsborough.

Hazards: Watch for traffic on village streets.

Rescue index: You're never more than a mile or two from a populated back road.

Land status: State forest, public roads

Maps: Pick up a trail map of Fox Forest at forest headquarters on Hillsborough Center Road, either before or during your ride.

Finding the trail: This ride starts from Grimes Field on Preston.

RIDE 6 · Fox Forest Loop

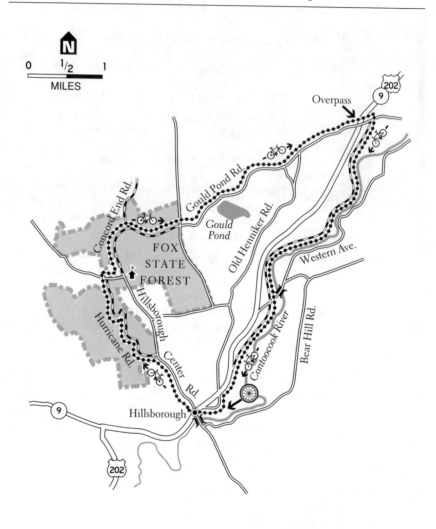

0   1/2   1
MILES

Overpass

202
9

Gould Pond Rd.

Gould
Pond

Old Henniker Rd.

Concord End Rd.

FOX
STATE
FOREST

Western Ave.

Hillsborough

Hurricane Rd.

Center Rd.

Contoocook River

Bear Hill Rd.

Hillsborough

9

202

Sources of additional information:

New Hampshire Division of Forests and Lands
P.O. Box 1856
172 Pembroke Road
Concord, NH 03302-1856
(603) 271-3456

Fox Forest manager
(603) 464-3453

Banagan's Cycling Company
27 South Main Street
Concord, NH 03301
(603) 225-3330
Employee James McDonough is the Hillsborough-area mountain bike oracle.

Notes on the trail: From Grimes Field take River Street past the trucks, turn right onto Bridge Street, and cross US 202/NH 9 at the traffic light. Take School Street for about a mile, past the school and the power lines. The first left turn after the cemetery entrance is Hurricane Road, a pleasant woods trail through Fox Forest. It returns you to the pavement after about 1.5 miles; turn right and then, shortly afterward, left onto Concord End Road (graded dirt).

You'll see the right turn for Gould Pond Road shortly after passing a small family cemetery. Gould Pond Road is the roughest part of the trip; watch for rocks and ruts during the descent. You'll exit the forest at Bog Road; the surface alternates between pavement and graded dirt for the next few miles before merging onto Old Hillsborough Road. Just after the bridge over the new alignment of US 202/NH 9, turn right onto an unmarked dirt road.

The surface is a bit rough in spots, and the trees sometimes close in tight, but this former railroad bed is level and mostly good. When you find yourself at the paved road, zig right, then zig left back onto the railroad bed again, then *stay straight* the rest of the way into town (even in spots where a well-worn trail branches off). Here the surface has worn into a wavy profile that's a blast to ride at high speeds.

The railroad bed ends at an auto-repair shop at the edge of Hillsborough. Thread your way through the used cars and down the shoulder of US 202/NH 9. Preston Street, the turnoff for Grimes Field, is about 1,000 feet ahead on the left.

RIDE 7 · Franklin Pierce Loop

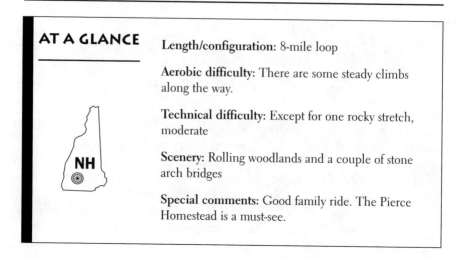

AT A GLANCE

Length/configuration: 8-mile loop

Aerobic difficulty: There are some steady climbs along the way.

Technical difficulty: Except for one rocky stretch, moderate

Scenery: Rolling woodlands and a couple of stone arch bridges

Special comments: Good family ride. The Pierce Homestead is a must-see.

You've seen that name before. Think back to fifth-grade American history: Zachary Taylor, Millard Fillmore . . . ah! Franklin Pierce, fourteenth president of the United States, of course! With so many presidential wanna-bes visiting the state every election year, it's hard to believe that only one native Granite Stater has ever made it to the White House (John Sununu doesn't count). Franklin and seven siblings grew up here in *this* white house on the Second New Hampshire Turnpike.

The Pierce Homestead is our starting point for an 8-mile loop that mixes pavement and graded dirt roads with a rugged piece of Class VI road. You'll also see a stone arch bridge or two along the way. Afterward, step into the homestead and learn a little about the lifestyle of New Hampshire's early politicians. The homestead looks rustic by contemporary standards, but remember that in the early nineteenth century, any home with clapboards and imported French wallpaper was pretty fancy stuff.

General location: South of Hillsborough on NH 31

Elevation change: About 500 feet of gain over several gradual climbs

Season: Late spring through fall

Services: Water, food, and lodging are in Hillsborough. A convenience store is at the corner of NH 9 and NH 31 near the start of the ride.

Hazards: Watch for light traffic on NH 31. One section of Gleason Falls Road is very eroded and rocky.

Rescue index: Most of this ride is on lightly populated back roads; assistance isn't far off.

Land status: Public roads

Maps: Page 26 of DeLorme's *New Hampshire Atlas and Gazetteer*. Also see Hillsboro and Hillsboro Upper Village quadrangles, USGS 7.5 minute series.

RIDE 7 · Franklin Pierce Loop

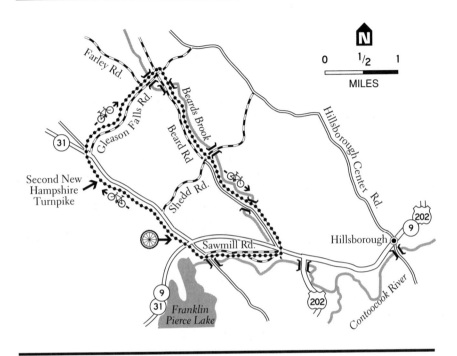

Finding the trail: Parking is available at the Pierce Homestead on NH 31 about 3 miles south of Hillsborough.

Source of additional information:

> The Hillsborough Historical Society
> P.O. Box 896
> Hillsborough, NH 03244
> The society operates the homestead and can be reached at (603) 478-3165.

Notes on the trail: Take NH 31 east and turn right onto Gleason Falls Road. This road starts out as graded dirt; after about a mile it becomes a rugged Class VI road, but not for long (only about 0.4 mile). When you see a graded dirt surface again, bear right down a short hill, then turn right onto Beard Road. You'll see the first stone arch bridge to your left, where pavement begins (continue straight on Beard). When you reach NH 9, cross the highway and bear right onto the dirt road (here's where you'll find the second stone arch bridge of this ride). The penstock (huge pipe) you see snaking through the woods carries the waters of Franklin Pierce Lake, of course. Continue straight when you rejoin the paved road; at the **T** intersection beyond, turn right onto NH 31. The Pierce Homestead lies just a half mile and one traffic light ahead of you.

Two dirt roads meet near the birthplace of America's fourteenth president.

RIDE 8 · Mink Hills

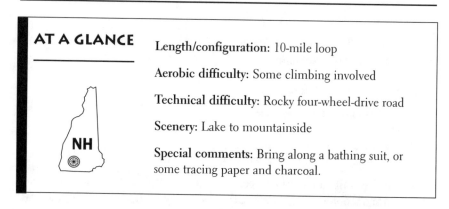

AT A GLANCE

NH

Length/configuration: 10-mile loop

Aerobic difficulty: Some climbing involved

Technical difficulty: Rocky four-wheel-drive road

Scenery: Lake to mountainside

Special comments: Bring along a bathing suit, or some tracing paper and charcoal.

Okay, the part about the bathing suit is obvious enough: the public beach on Lake Massasecum is close by. After a tough climb on double-track, a swooping descent on dirt, and a speedy return on the highway, you're gonna be dirty and sticky. What better way to wash off the mud, dead bugs, and other encrusted trail matter than a refreshing dip? If you'd like to put your arms instead of your legs to use for a while, rental boats are available, too.

What about the tracing paper and charcoal? Along this ride, you'll pass by several abandoned farms, as evidenced by the stone fences, cellar holes, and large,

RIDE 8 · Mink Hills

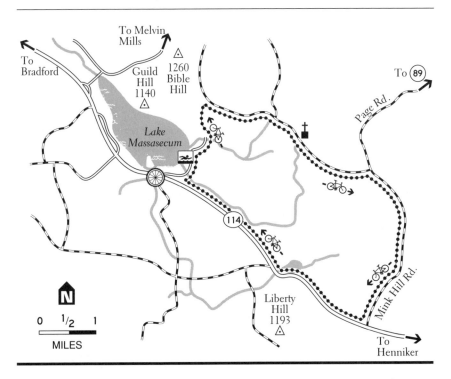

hardwood trees. Along the way lies one of New Hampshire's forgotten rural cemeteries with the kind of gravestones you won't find at the local Rock of Ages showroom. Take a break from the ride, find a stone with an inscription or design that moves you, and make a rubbing to take home.

General location: 6 miles north of Henniker on NH 114

Elevation change: A 500-foot climb and corresponding descent

Season: Late spring through fall

Services: Lake Massasecum Casino Park Campground, (603) 938-2571, offers food and campsites. Other services can be found in Henniker, 6 miles to the south, and Bradford, 3 miles to the north.

Hazards: Watch for loose rocks when descending on the four-wheel-drive road.

Rescue index: You are within a mile of populated areas at all times.

Land status: Public roads

Maps: Page 26 of DeLorme's *New Hampshire Atlas and Gazetteer*

Finding the trail: Park at the boat-launch site on NH 114, 5.3 miles north of US 202/NH 9 and across from the campground entrance.

Source of additional information:

Banagan's Cycling Company
27 South Main Street
Concord, NH 03301
(603) 225-3330
Ask to speak with employee James McDonough—he's the Hillsborough-area
mountain bike guru.

Notes on the trail: Take the paved access road along the shore of Lake
Massasecum and turn left just after the public beach. A half mile beyond, you'll
see a sandy road on the right—take it and start climbing. The road becomes a
trail and continues to climb. At the **T** intersection, turn right. After about a mile,
the road forks; bear right and watch for the cemetery. Ride for another mile, bear
left, and almost immediately make a sharp right. A long descent begins here; be
sure to watch out for the rocks. At the bottom, turn right onto NH 114 and return
to the boat launch on its very ridable paved shoulder.

RIDE 9 · Pillsbury State Park

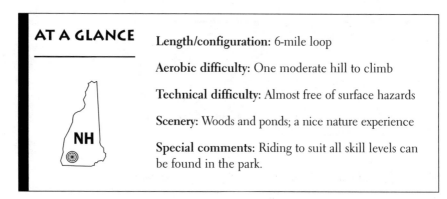

AT A GLANCE

Length/configuration: 6-mile loop

Aerobic difficulty: One moderate hill to climb

Technical difficulty: Almost free of surface hazards

Scenery: Woods and ponds; a nice nature experience

Special comments: Riding to suit all skill levels can
be found in the park.

NH

Pillsbury State Park is 5,500 acres of undulating wilderness with some large
ponds, campground facilities, and a generous network of trails—easy, flat
trails and tough, rocky ones. I wound up riding one of each; the ride described
here is the easy, flat one.

(For those curious: the other was the Pamac Trail, which gets progressively harder. After three miles, I turned back in favor of an all-you-can-eat
spaghetti supper at the grange hall in Goshen—everything homemade, except
for the spaghetti, sauce, pickles, Kool-Aid, and the whipped topping on the
brownies. Delicious! An advanced biker can, I'm told, bushwhack all the way to

RIDE 9 · Pillsbury State Park

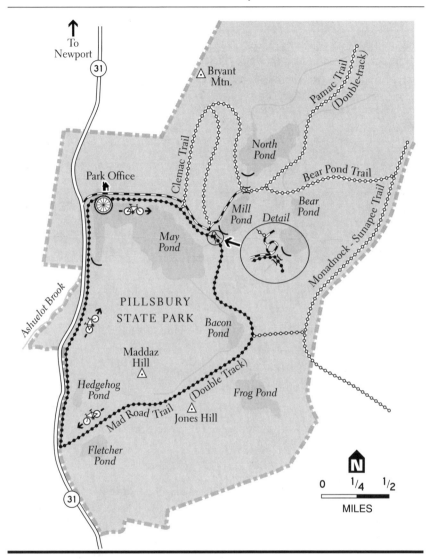

To
Newport

31

Bryant
Mtn.

Parnac Trail
(Double-track)

North
Pond

Clemac Trail

Bear Pond Trail

Park Office

Mill
Pond   Detail

Bear
Pond

Monadnock - Sunapee Trail

May
Pond

Ashuelot Brook

PILLSBURY
STATE PARK   Bacon
Pond

Maddaz
Hill

Hedgehog
Pond

Mad Road Trail   (Double Track)

Frog Pond

Jones Hill

Fletcher
Pond

31

N

0   1/4   1/2

MILES

Mount Sunapee State Park via the Monadnock-Sunapee Greenway, which travels entirely through state parks and adjoining conservation easements.)

This ride follows the Mad Road Trail around the lower reaches of the park and past several ponds, in a mostly wooded area. At trail's end, a short ride up NH 31 takes you back to the park entrance.

General location: 4 miles north of Washington on NH 31

One of the easy flat trails in Pillsbury State Park.

Elevation change: Less than 200 feet of climbing throughout the ride

Season: Late spring through fall

Services: Camping and water are available within the park. Other services are available in Newport, 9 miles north on NH 31.

Hazards: NH 31 is a winding, shoulderless highway. Watch for moderate traffic.

Rescue index: You are within 2 miles of assistance throughout the ride.

Land status: State park

Maps: A trail map is available free at the park office.

Finding the trail: Park at the office, which is about a half mile in from the park entrance.

Source of additional information:

New Hampshire Division of Parks and Recreation, Parks Bureau
P.O. Box 1856
172 Pembroke Road
Concord, NH 03302-1856
(603) 271-3556

Notes on the trail: Take the park's main dirt road for just over a mile. Just past the gray barn, hang a right onto a trail that takes you past the outhouses and over the bridge. Keep right; this is the Mad Road Trail. It's like a good Class VI road, rustic but very ridable, and it lasts for about 2.5 miles. At the end, turn right onto NH 31 and ride about 1.8 miles to the park entrance.

RIDE 10 · Mount Sunapee State Park

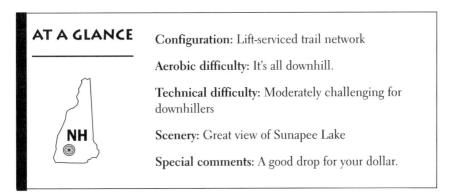

AT A GLANCE

Configuration: Lift-serviced trail network

Aerobic difficulty: It's all downhill.

Technical difficulty: Moderately challenging for downhillers

Scenery: Great view of Sunapee Lake

Special comments: A good drop for your dollar.

NH

The mountain biking at Mount Sunapee's ski facilities has a disturbingly tentative feel to it. The brochures are circulating, the lift is running, and trails are marked, but the schedules are limited, and actual bikers are few. Management seems to be taking a wait-and-see attitude before making significant investments in mountain bike trails. Meanwhile, mountain bikers are taking a wait-and-see attitude before hitting the lift in great numbers.

I hope the standoff ends before Sunapee gives it up. Anyone who enjoys downhilling will want to give the place a try. There are only two trails open, but they're good ones, with a respectable 1,500-foot drop. Because it's a state-owned facility, the park's all-day lift ticket is about the cheapest around. They don't rent mountain bikes on-site, but the bike shop just outside the park entrance does. Sunapee also happens to be closer to New England's urban centers than any other lift-serviced trail in this book.

General location: 2 miles west of Newbury on NH 103

Elevation change: 1,500 feet of vertical drop from the summit

Season: Open daily, July 1 to September 1. Rates (in 1997): $8, single ride; $15, all day.

Services: Bike rentals and repair are available at Bob Skinner's Ski and Sport on NH 103, just east of the traffic circle, (603) 763-2303. Other services can be found in Newport or Bradford, 3 miles east on NH 103.

Hazards: Watch for waterbars across the trails, and don't let your speed get out of control.

Rescue index: Trails signed for mountain biking are patrolled.

Land status: State-owned downhill ski facility

Maps: A black-and-white contour map comes with your lift ticket.

Finding the trail: The entrance to Mount Sunapee is just off the traffic circle at NH 103 and NH 103A, and prominently signed.

RIDE 10 · Mount Sunapee State Park

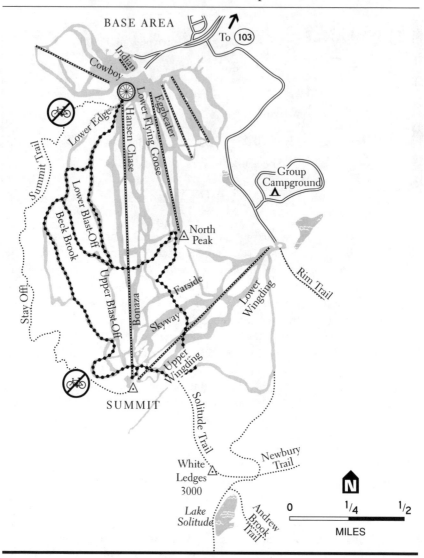

Source of additional information:

Mount Sunapee State Park
(603) 763-2356

Notes on the trail: Coming off the lift, walk your bike down the stairs to the trailhead. As mentioned above, you have two trail choices: "longer" and "faster." Signage is skimpy but adequate, and trail maintenance is good (one steep stretch had been thoughtfully covered with wood chips). Check your brakes, then let 'er rip.

RIDE 11 · Newbury Cut

AT A GLANCE

Length/configuration: 6.5-mile out-and-back (3.3 miles each way)

Aerobic difficulty: Couldn't be easier

Technical difficulty: Just a few sandy spots

Scenery: Woods and rocks

Special comments: Newbury Cut is hailed as a marvel of nineteenth-century civil engineering.

NH

Were it not for a fire in a Montreal roundhouse decades ago, this piece of the former Concord and Claremont Railroad might still be running trains. The operator of a local tourist train couldn't produce paperwork for his Canadian-built steam locomotive, so the feds shut him down in 1961, thus dooming the line. (Ironically, the tourist operation wound up in Pennsylvania as the government's much-maligned Steamtown National Historic Site.)

In his book *Through Covered Bridges to Concord*, Edgar T. Mead, Jr. describes the construction of Newbury Cut in 1871: "A new-fangled steam drill was brought to bear, aimed at removing 10,000 feet of vicious conglomerate rock. The monster's chief weapon was a 2.5-inch bit. A full head of steam inched it forward at the rate of 9 feet in 50 minutes—rocketing progress compared to hand methods. Ten-pound charges of black powder reduced the conglomerate to fragments that could then be used on the graceful, spiraling grades up out of the valley floor several hundred feet below."

And you thought *you* had it tough on National Trails Day.

General location: Newbury

Elevation change: Negligible

Season: Mid-spring to fall

Services: All services can be found in Newbury, or in Bradford, 3 miles to the east.

Hazards: Watch for some sandy patches on the trail. Avoid riding on adjacent private land.

Rescue index: You're never more than a mile from the highway.

Land status: Town-owned railroad bed (adjacent land is privately owned).

Maps: None necessary, really, but if you insist, try the Newport sheet, USGS 7.5 × 15 minute series.

Finding the trail: Park at the Newbury town dock's parking lot on NH 103, right near the information booth. The trail begins behind the Trading Post.

RIDE 11 · Newbury Cut

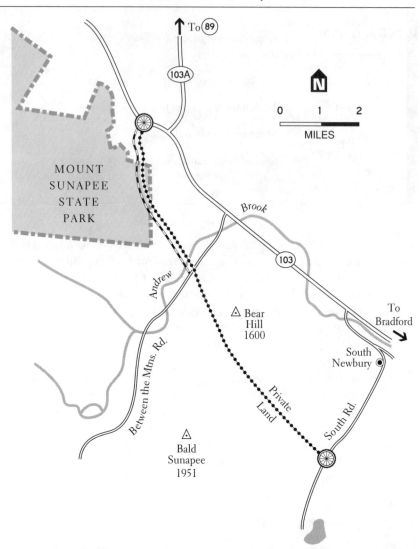

Source of additional information:

Outspokin' Bicycle and Sport Shop
P.O. Box 264
889 Route 103
Newbury, NH 03255
(603) 763-9500
Proprietor Will Hurley is the leading expert on mountain biking in the area.

RIDE 12 · Sugar River Trail

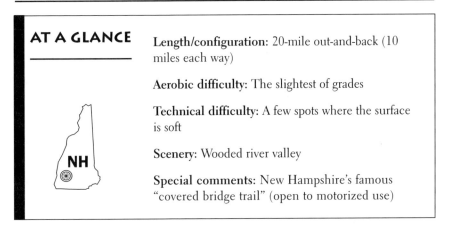

AT A GLANCE

Length/configuration: 20-mile out-and-back (10 miles each way)

Aerobic difficulty: The slightest of grades

Technical difficulty: A few spots where the surface is soft

Scenery: Wooded river valley

Special comments: New Hampshire's famous "covered bridge trail" (open to motorized use)

There are people who make a hobby of spotting covered bridges. They scour maps for locations, plan their vacations around it, and keep "life lists" just like birdwatchers do. New Hampshire even prints brochures and puts up signs for their benefit.

If you know any of these folks and would like to ease their transition into a *real* leisure-time activity (like, say . . . mountain biking), be sure to tell them about this rail trail. It features not one, but *two*, covered bridges (and some cool steel bridges as well). They're not just ordinary covered bridges, either: they're *railroad* covered bridges, of the Double Web Town-Pratt lattice design (don't worry, they'll know what it means), built in 1871 for the Sugar River Railroad and used for nearly a century.

So why were covered bridges *covered*, anyway? A lot of myth and romanticism surrounds this question; the simple answer is that the roof kept the structural timbers dry, thus preventing rot. Close inspection of the two covered bridges along this trail will tell you that the strategy worked—they've held up better than many steel bridges of more recent vintage.

General location: Newport

Elevation change: Negligible

Season: Mid-spring through fall

Services: All services can be found in Newport and Claremont, the ends of the trail.

Hazards: Watch for soft, sandy surfaces in spots, and for light traffic at grade crossings.

Rescue index: You're always within a mile of traveled roads and populated areas.

Land status: State-owned railroad bed

RIDE 12 · Sugar River Trail

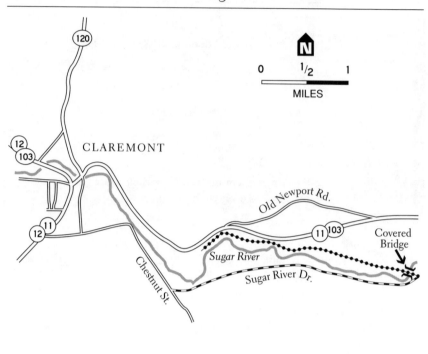

Maps: A brochure with small maps of this and five other multiuse trails is available from the New Hampshire Division of Parks and Recreation, Bureau of Trails.

Finding the trail: From the town square in Newport, take Main Street north a few blocks to Belknap Avenue and turn left. A large parking area on your right features a signboard for the trail.

Source of additional information:

New Hampshire Division of Parks and Recreation, Trails Bureau
P.O. Box 1856
172 Pembroke Road
Concord, NH 03302-1856
(603) 271-3254

Notes on the trail: From Newport, the trail first swings northward, following the Sugar River on a broad arc to Kellyville. Here the trail is wooded and secluded. The trail passes underneath the NH 11/103 highway bridge at Kellyville—at roughly the halfway point. About 1.5 miles beyond you'll encounter the first of the covered bridges. The trail then meets a dirt road.

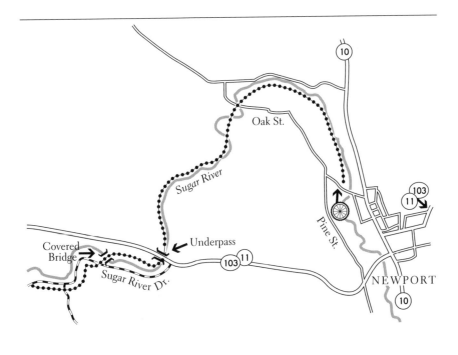

Although the railroad bed can be found on the south shoulder of the road, it's rough here. Use the road instead until the trail diverges to the right (about 0.5 mile). The second covered bridge is about 800 feet down the trail from the road.

For now, the trail ends at a parking area on NH 11/103, about a half mile from the outskirts of Claremont. An additional section of railroad bed is currently being prepared, to extend the trail closer to the shopping plazas along NH 11/103. Watch for traffic if you decide to take the highway into the village.

MERRIMACK
(SOUTHEASTERN NEW HAMPSHIRE)

This section encompasses New Hampshire's seacoast, its industrial area, and its capitol district—what those farther north refer to as the flatlands. New Hampshire was first settled here, the settlers working their way gradually northward later. The cities of Nashua, Manchester, and Concord have grown up along strategic points on the Merrimack River. Rochester and Dover have claimed sites along tributaries of the Piscataqua, and Portsmouth has staked its claim where the Piscataqua meets the sea. Before the interstates, before the Public Service Company of New Hampshire, before the Boston & Maine Railway, these rivers provided power and transportation to New Hampshire's mills. Even though much of the shipbuilding and the textiles and shoe manufacturing have since drifted away, manufacturing remains a driving force in the lower region of the state.

Fifty years ago, writer John Gunther described Concord as "the ugliest state capitol I ever saw." Since then, some of the buildings surrounding the statehouse have given way to more harmonious structures, but downtown Concord retains much of its ad hoc appearance. Surprisingly, few buildings are constructed of the Granite State's native stone. The product of the region's quarries is regarded as a cash crop; locals prefer to build with bricks or clapboards.

Here in the flatlands, the mountain biking is easier and enjoys a riding season longer than that of the higher elevations to the north. Other bikers are easy to find, and some of the bike shops are even open on Sundays.

Suggested Reading: *Yankee Kingdom* by Ralph Nading Hill. A lively account of the history of New Hampshire (and neighboring Vermont) from colonial settlements to the twentieth century. You'll learn why such a small state has such a large legislature, what made Mary Baker Eddy (a Granite State native who founded the Christian Science church) such a controversial figure, and how Beloit, Wisconsin, figures in New Hampshire's past.

RIDE 13 · Potanipo Hill

AT A GLANCE

NH

Length/configuration: 7-mile loop

Aerobic difficulty: Moderate; several short climbs

Technical difficulty: Easy

Scenery: Good birdwatching from Potanipo Hill

Special comments: Bring your binoculars.

I'm still trying to figure out why "single-track" is such a Holy Grail to so many mountain bikers. Bikers will argue over whether a given stretch of bumpy trail is "real" single-track or not, and frankly, some trails awarded the Single-Track Seal of Approval aren't much fun to ride. Real, honest-to-goodness single-track is hard to find, especially in the lower reaches of New Hampshire, where the hills are low and the valleys settled and developed.

There's not a foot of single-track on this ride. So what? Anyone can ride it; the surroundings are scenic; and the wildlife-watching opportunities along the way are pretty good. What more do you really need for a good ride?

General location: Brookline

Elevation change: About 900 feet of altitude gain, in several ascents

Season: Late spring through fall

Services: All services are available in Brookline, and in Milford, 9 miles north on NH 13.

Hazards: Watch for light traffic on Brookline Road and occasional muddy spots in the woods.

Rescue index: You're within a mile of populated areas at all times.

Land status: Public roads

Maps: Page 21 of DeLorme's *New Hampshire Atlas and Gazetteer*. Also see Townsend, Massachusetts, quadrangle, USGS 7.5 minute series.

Finding the trail: From Milford, take NH 13 south for about 7.5 miles and turn west onto Brookline Road (the intersection is about 1 mile beyond NH 130; the Massachusetts state line lies about 2.5 miles farther south). Immediately after turning onto Brookline Road, you'll see a wide area on the left next to the bridge where you can park.

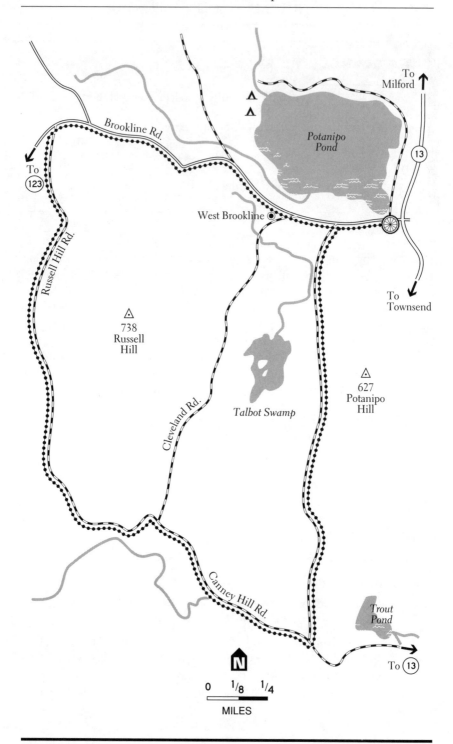

To Milford

Potanipo Pond

Brookline Rd.

To 123

West Brookline

13

Russell Hill Rd.

To Townsend

738 Russell Hill

Cleveland Rd.

Talbot Swamp

627 Potanipo Hill

Canney Hill Rd.

Trout Pond

To 13

N

0   1/8   1/4

MILES

Sources of additional information: Any friendly birdwatcher you happen to meet along the way

Notes on the trail: From your parking spot, take Brookline Road a few hundred feet farther and turn left onto a double-track trail. This will take you to the summit of Potanipo Hill and a great view of the countryside. Descend and turn right onto the paved road. Ride for about a mile, then bear left onto a gravel road. At the next fork, bear right, and follow the double-track trail into the woods. A leisurely ride across the slope of Russell Hill will eventually take you down to Brookline Road. Turn right and ride the remaining 1.5 miles back to the start.

RIDE 14 · Beaver Brook

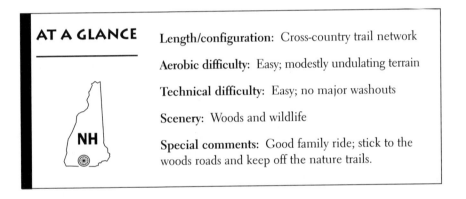

AT A GLANCE

Length/configuration: Cross-country trail network

Aerobic difficulty: Easy; modestly undulating terrain

Technical difficulty: Easy; no major washouts

Scenery: Woods and wildlife

Special comments: Good family ride; stick to the woods roads and keep off the nature trails.

Stone fences are a New England tradition. If you've done much riding in New Hampshire so far, doubtless you've noticed that virtually every dirt road in the state is lined with an old stone fence about knee-high delineating a pasture that's long since gone back to the trees. Back when agriculture played a much bigger role in New Hampshire's economy, stone fences were an economical means of keeping the livestock close to home, as well as a handy way to dispose of all the big rocks that the state's farmland is so famous for. Robert Frost devoted a poem to the annual ritual of mending stone fences, which gave rise to the immortal quote, "Good fences make good neighbors." (The line is spoken by the narrator's neighbor in response to this verse, rarely quoted: "My apple trees will never get across / And eat the cones under his pines, I tell him.")

The roads here in the Beaver Brook Wildlife Habitat are, of course, lined with stone fences, but they're not the main attraction. Beaver Brook has an educational center with exhibits on the progression of a New England forest, from weeds to

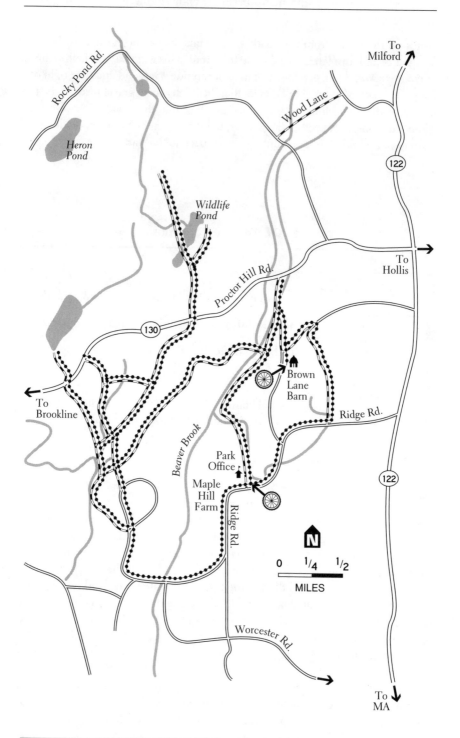

To Milford

Rocky Pond Rd.

Wood Lane

Heron Pond

122

Wildlife Pond

To Hollis

Proctor Hill Rd.

130

Brown Lane Barn

To Brookline

Beaver Brook

Ridge Rd.

Park Office

Maple Hill Farm

Ridge Rd.

122

N

0   1/4   1/2

MILES

Worcester Rd.

To MA

towering hardwoods. The natural process takes about 40 years; you can learn it all here in a couple of hours before or after your ride.

General location: Between Brookline and Hollis on NH 130

Elevation change: Minimal; there are some short climbs on the trails.

Season: Late spring through fall. The nature centers are open seven days a week.

Services: Water is available at the nature centers. Food, lodging, and camping can be found in the Hollis area along NH 122. A large bike shop, Goodale's Bike & Ski, is located at 46 Main Street in nearby Nashua, phone (603) 882-2111.

Hazards: Watch for pedestrians and other trail users, and keep an eye out for minor surface hazards.

Rescue index: You are within a half mile of assistance at all times.

Land status: Privately run wildlife habitat. Bicycling is permitted on the broad woods roads—please stay off the narrower hiking trails.

Maps: A map is available for a nominal charge at either the Maple Hill Farm office or the Brown Lane Barn.

Finding the trail: From Hollis, take NH 122 south for 1 mile and turn right onto Ridge Road. Maple Hill Farm, where the Beaver Brook Association offices are located, is about 1 mile beyond, on the right.

Source of additional information:

Beaver Brook Association
117 Ridge Road
Hollis, NH 03049
(603) 465-7787

Notes on the trail: After you've stopped into Maple Hill Farm for a map (and a look at the nature exhibits), hit the trails and have fun. (Remember, though: please stay off the designated nature trails.)

RIDE 15 · Hollis Town Forest

AT A GLANCE

NH

Length/configuration: Cross-country trail network

Aerobic difficulty: Easy

Technical difficulty: Easy to moderate woods trails

Scenery: Wooded

Special comments: Swimming is available across the road at Silver Lake State Park.

Time did not permit me to find out why so many New Hampshire towns are blessed with town forests. Maybe it's a remnant of some colonial tradition brought over by the British. It could be the result of a pioneering conservation effort demanded by the Granite State's many outdoors lovers. Perhaps the state tempts landowners with a break from its notorious property taxes (with no state sales or income tax, Concord's gotta get its money from somewhere). I intend to find out the first chance I get, because it's a great system that provides plenty of spots for mountain biking all over the state.

Hollis Town Forest (which is also known to some as the Dunklee Pond Conservation Area) is one of these little marvels. It's not big, but it's laced with a network of trails for hiking and cross-country skiing that also make dandy mountain bike trails.

General location: Hollis

Elevation change: Minimal; the terrain is relatively flat.

Season: Late spring through fall

Services: Water is available at the nearby Silver Lake State Park. Food, lodging, and camping are available near Hollis along NH 122. Goodale's Bike & Ski Shop is located at 46 Main Street in nearby Nashua, phone (603) 882-2111.

Hazards: Watch for occasional hikers and equestrians.

Rescue index: You are within a mile of inhabited areas.

Land status: Town forest

Maps: None available (or necessary)

Finding the trail: From Hollis take NH 122 north (follow the signs for Silver Lake State Park). About 1.2 miles beyond, there is a large gravel parking area on the right, across the road from the beach.

RIDE 15 · Hollis Town Forest

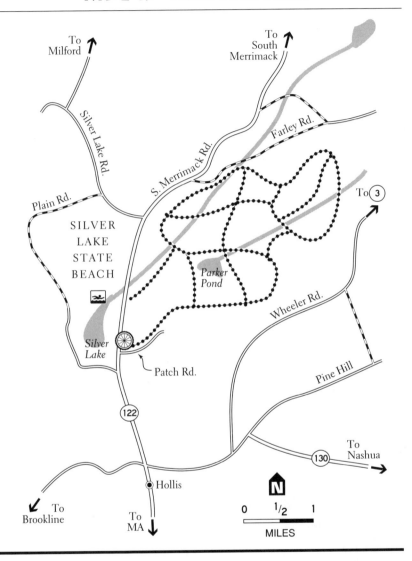

Source of additional information:

Hollis Town Hall
(603) 465-2209

Notes on the trail: From the parking area, follow NH 122 south a few hundred feet, take the first left turn onto Patch Road, ride another short distance, and bear left at the loop. About halfway around on the left is a gated trail into the forest. Once inside, explore the trails as the fancy strikes you.

RIDE 16 · Newfields Trail

AT A GLANCE

Length/configuration: 25-mile end-to-end

Aerobic difficulty: Flat riding throughout

Technical difficulty: Mostly devoid of surface hazards

Scenery: Towns and countryside in the seacoast region

Special comments: Open the throttle wide, and be sure to whistle at the crossings.

This is by far the longest continuous stretch of off-road riding in southern New Hampshire. (Throw in the connection to the Rockingham Recreational Trail [see below] and it gets even longer!) You guessed it—it's another rail trail, abandoned by the Boston & Maine Railway in the early 1980s and thoughtfully preserved for you by the State of New Hampshire. Unlike many of the state's rail trails, this one isn't opened to motorcycles or ATVs. There's no distracting two-cycle racket to drown out the chugging noises you make as you barrel along, pretending to be a Boston & Maine Class B-15 Mogul steam locomotive hauling the afternoon local to Portsmouth.

General location: Between Newfields and Manchester

Elevation change: Negligible

Season: Spring through fall (and winter, if you're so inclined and equipped)

Services: Food and water can be had at convenience stores on intersecting roads. Banagan's Cycling Company is located at 320 South Willow Street in Manchester, phone (603) 623-3330.

Hazards: Yield to traffic at all highway crossings. (Darn!)

Rescue index: You are within a mile of inhabited areas and traveled roads at all times.

Land status: State-owned abandoned railroad bed

Maps: Pages 28–29 of DeLorme's *New Hampshire Atlas and Gazetteer*

Finding the trail: The eastern trailhead is on NH 108 in Newfields, a half mile north of the junction with NH 85. Just north of the bridge on the west side is a paved access road to the abandoned railroad station. The trail begins behind the station, heading away from the remaining railroad tracks.

The western trailhead is east of Manchester on NH Bypass 28, just south of the traffic circle with NH 121. Park along the road near the playing fields.

The trail can also be accessed at any intersecting road along its length (most have wide dirt areas for parking).

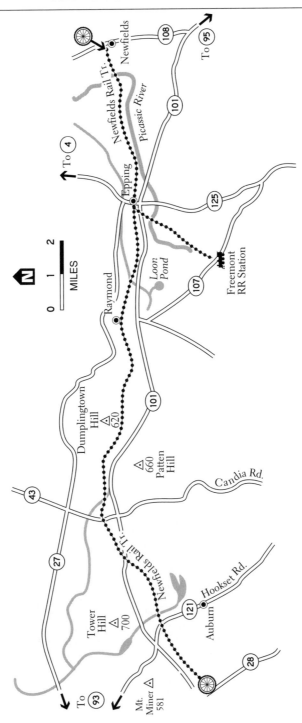

Sources of additional information:

New Hampshire Division of Parks and Recreation, Trails Bureau
P.O. Box 1856
172 Pembroke Road
Concord, NH 03302-1856
(603) 271-3254

Wheel Power
183 Water Street
Exeter, NH 03833
(603) 772-6343

Notes on the trail: As is typical on rail trails, the riding is pretty easy here. You may lose the trail at some of the highway crossings, but rest assured that it's there, possibly disguised as a driveway or an access road. Cross the highway and look for a straight, level dirt road that continues in the same direction you were riding.

In Epping, another trail branches off in a southwesterly direction toward Fremont Station, four miles away. This is the connector to the Rockingham Recreational Trail (see next ride).

RIDE 17 · Rockingham Recreational Trail

AT A GLANCE

Length/configuration: 14-mile end-to-end, with optional 4-mile extension

Aerobic difficulty: Level riding throughout

Technical difficulty: Sandy trail conditions

Scenery: Semiwooded countryside with ponds and wetlands

NH

Special comments: This trail is open to motorized use.

If you love the scent of burning two-cycle oil, this is the ride for you. It's a state-owned rail trail that's open to motorcycles and ATVers, as well as nonmotorized folks like you. While that might *sound* dangerous, it's not. The trail is wide, and sight distance is excellent throughout. On the sunny autumn Sunday of my ride, there were many ATVs on the trail. They behaved quite well in my presence, slowing down and keeping to the other side as they passed. Administrators at the state's Bureau of Trails report no problems with bike-ATV conflicts.

Not far from Windham Depot (about two miles off the trail) is the Robert Frost Farm State Historic Site. Frost owned farms all over New Hampshire and

RIDE 17 · Rockingham Recreational Trail

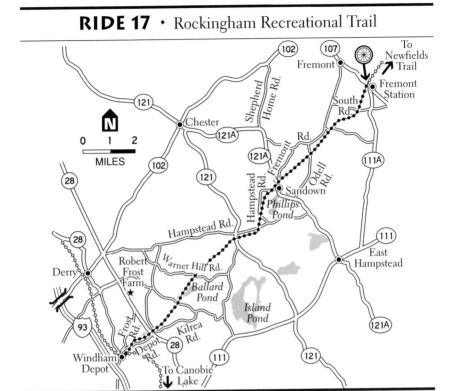

adjoining states, leaving behind a dizzying array of authentic historic sites, each with its own cast-iron marker. He lived on this particular Robert Frost Farm as a young family man for ten years, before sailing to England in 1912. It's open to the public on limited weekend hours.

General location: Between Derry and Fremont

Elevation change: Negligible

Season: Spring through fall (and winter, for those mountain bikers "Stopping by Woods on a Snowy Evening")

Services: Food and lodging are available in Derry. Camping can be found in the Hampstead area (south of the trail on NH 121). For bicycle needs, try Banagan's Cycling Company, 320 South Willow Street, Manchester, NH 03103, (603) 623-3330.

Hazards: Keep an ear out for approaching ATVs. Watch for traffic at highway crossings. Be prepared to ride through some areas with soft, sandy surfaces.

Rescue index: The trail is frequently crossed by traveled roads, and inhabited areas are generally within a mile.

A perfect day on the
Rockingham
Recreational Trail—
sunny, and not a
Kawasaki in sight.

Land status: State-owned railroad bed

Maps: A brochure with small maps of this and five other multiuse trails is available from the New Hampshire Division of Parks and Recreation, Bureau of Trails.

Finding the trail: The eastern trailhead is a mile south of Fremont, on NH 107. The former railroad station, now a private residence, sits on the west side of the highway, and the railroad bed is clearly visible on both sides. A dirt parking area is provided on the east side of the highway. East of this point, the railroad grade is off-limits to motorcycles and ATVs, but you can bike on it to reach the Newfields Trail (see Ride 16).

The western trailhead is at Windham Depot. From Derry take NH 28 south for about 3.5 miles and turn right on Depot Road. About 1.5 miles beyond, there is a crossroads; Windham Depot is a cluster of white buildings on your left. (You'll see two rail trails behind the old depot. The one toward Fremont is on the left. The trail on the right goes southeast toward Canobie Lake and can be ridden as an optional 8-mile out-and-back.)

Source of additional information:

New Hampshire Division of Parks and Recreation, Trails Bureau
P.O. Box 1856
172 Pembroke Road
Concord, NH 03302-1856
(603) 271-3254

Notes on the trail: The trail surface is frequently sandy, and in some spots, *very* sandy. Folks riding not-so-fat tires and expecting a typical hard-pack rail-to-trail conversion are going to be disappointed here. The ATV traffic has churned up the surface, to be sure, but the railroad bed wasn't really built up for recreational use to begin with. (Portions of this trail were abandoned by the railroad as long ago as 1935.) State officials hope to correct the problem in the future.

RIDE 18 · Pawtuckaway State Park

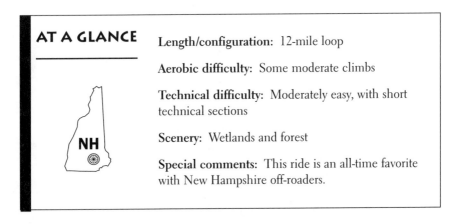

AT A GLANCE

Length/configuration: 12-mile loop

Aerobic difficulty: Some moderate climbs

Technical difficulty: Moderately easy, with short technical sections

Scenery: Wetlands and forest

Special comments: This ride is an all-time favorite with New Hampshire off-roaders.

NH

Ask a native New Hampshire mountain biker where to ride—invariably, Pawtuckaway comes up. Maybe it's the convenience to Concord and Manchester, with easy access via NH 101 and US 4. Maybe it's the generous 5,500-acre size, with the variety of landscapes from marshland to wooded hill to rocky cliff. Perhaps it's the swimming and camping on-site. Or the chance to see a great blue heron along the lake. Or a name that rolls off the tongue so much more smoothly than, say, Massabesic or Piscataqua do.

I'm guessing, though, that it's got something to do with the trails. There's a lot of them, ranging from easy to fairly challenging, and with certain exceptions (due to heavy hiking traffic in the summer season), they're all open to mountain bikes.

RIDE 18 · Pawtuckaway State Park

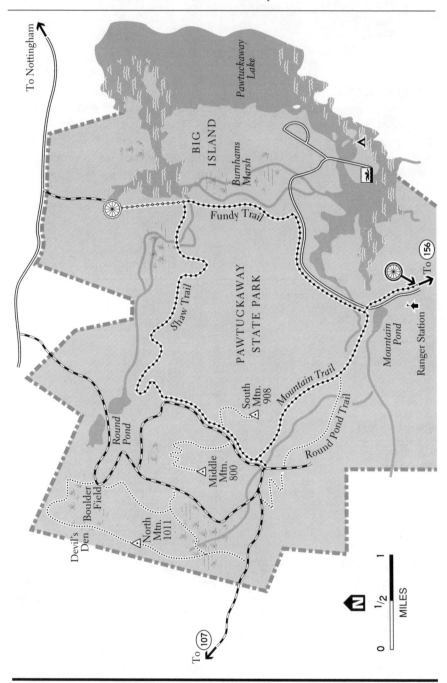

To Nottingham

Pawtuckaway Lake

BIG ISLAND

Burnhams Marsh

Fundy Trail

Shaw Trail

PAWTUCKAWAY STATE PARK

South Mtn. 908

Mountain Trail

Round Pond

Round Pond Trail

Mountain Pond

To 156

Ranger Station

Middle Mtn. 800

Devil's Den

Boulder Field

North Mtn. 1011

To 107

N

0   1/2   1

MILES

No name rolls off a
mountain biker's tongue
more readily than
"Pawtuckaway."

General location: Nottingham

Elevation change: Mostly flat, with a couple of climbs of about 120 feet each

Season: Spring through fall. (Local mountain bikers also ride during the winter.)

Services: Water and camping are available on-site. Other services can be found in Nottingham or in Raymond, 3 miles south on NH 156.

Hazards: Watch for hikers and various surface hazards on single-track trails.

Rescue index: You are within a mile of traveled park roads at all times.

Land status: State park. (Some park trails are closed to bicyclists during summer weekends. Inquire at the park information center.)

Maps: A trail map is available at the park information center.

Finding the trail: From Exit 5 off NH 101, take NH 156 north for about 1.5 miles, following the brown state park signs. Turn left onto Mountain Road; the entrance to the park is about one mile ahead on the left. There is a small admission fee during the summer season.

Source of additional information:

> New Hampshire Division of Parks and Recreation, Parks Bureau
> P.O. Box 1856
> 172 Pembroke Road
> Concord, NH 03302-1856
> (603) 271-3556
> The park manager can be reached at (603) 895-3031.

Notes on the trail: From the parking area, take the paved road past the toll booth, turn right, and follow the pavement downhill for about a mile. Watch for the Fundy Trail, a four-wheel-drive dirt road, on the left. Follow it over a wooden bridge, past a wetland, and to a **T** intersection. Turn left onto the Shaw Trail and follow it for a couple of miles, until you reach the road. Turn left (a right turn here takes you on a side trip to Devil's Den, about three-quarters of a mile off).

Follow the road and watch for the Mountain Trail, which branches off to the left where the road swings right. The Mountain Trail takes you across the southern reaches of the park and ends at the paved road you traveled early in the ride. Turn right and climb the hill to return to your starting point.

RIDE 19 · Massabesic Lake

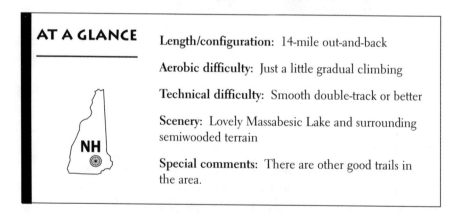

AT A GLANCE

Length/configuration: 14-mile out-and-back

Aerobic difficulty: Just a little gradual climbing

Technical difficulty: Smooth double-track or better

Scenery: Lovely Massabesic Lake and surrounding semiwooded terrain

Special comments: There are other good trails in the area.

Manchester, the largest city in New Hampshire, is a good place for an outdoor lover to call home, and Massabesic Lake, just four miles from the heart of downtown, is the reason why. On its shore sits a municipal park with baseball diamonds, tennis courts, and, of course, picnic tables. The lake itself is a popular spot for canoeing and birdwatching. And let's not forget those trails!

This ride takes you over some of those trails and up to Tower Hill Pond, a reservoir that supplies the city's water. Additional trails around the lake and pond

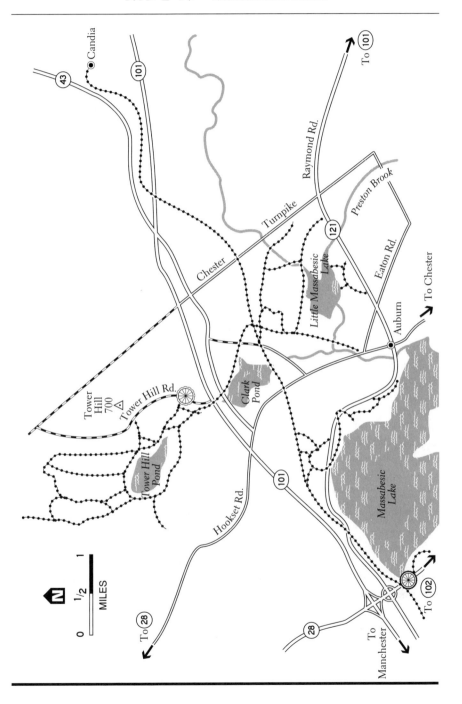

await your exploration as well. Some local cyclists even continue on Snowmobile Route 15 up to Bear Brook State Park (Ride 21); if you're feeling ambitious, inquire locally for directions.

General location: East of Manchester on NH Bypass 28

Elevation change: The ride is flat most of the way, with some gradual climbs.

Season: Spring through fall (and winter, if you're so inclined and equipped)

Services: Water is available at the trailhead (near the baseball fields). The nearest convenience store is located just north of the trailhead. Other services are located in Manchester.

Hazards: Watch for other trail users, especially on weekends.

Rescue index: You are within a mile of inhabited areas or traveled roads at all times.

Land status: State-owned railroad bed, and utility service roads

Maps: Candia quadrangle, USGS 7.5 minute series

Finding the trail: From Exit 1 on NH 101, take NH Bypass 28 south for a short distance. Just beyond the traffic circle is the trailhead (on the left, opposite the baseball fields). Park along the road.

Sources of additional information:

New Hampshire Division of Parks and Recreation, Trails Bureau
P.O. Box 1856
172 Pembroke Road
Concord, NH 03302-1856
(603) 271-3254

Banagan's Cycling Company
320 South Willow Street
Manchester, NH 03103
(603) 623-3330

Notes on the trail: From the trailhead, take the rail trail east along the north shore of the lake (this is the western end of Ride 16, the Newfields Trail). After about 3.2 miles, turn left onto a trail marked "Route 15 North" (it's a snowmobile route designation). The trail crosses a dirt road, then a paved one, then ducks under an underpass. Immediately beyond this, bear left onto a trail that climbs a short, steep hill, then turn left. Tower Hill Pond is now before you. Make a loop around it on the access road, then retrace the trail back to your starting point.

RIDE 20 · Hopkinton-Everett Lake Project

AT A GLANCE	Length/configuration: ATV trail network
	Aerobic difficulty: Moderate; some short, sharp hills
	Technical difficulty: Moderate to difficult
NH	Scenery: Wetlands, woods, and meadows
	Special comments: This trail is open to motor ized use.

Where would we mountain bikers be without the many large governmental agencies that manage land, construct roads and trails, and prevent large chunks of this country from being turned into subdivisions and shopping malls? In the case of the riding here, the organization to thank is one not usually associated with outdoor recreation: the U.S. Army Corps of Engineers. A few decades ago, the army put up this massive flood-control project along a tributary of the Contoocook River. Recreational use of "Hop-Ev" is now managed by the state's parks and recreation people. It's intended primarily as an ATV area, but mountain bikers are welcome to share it, and state officials report no user-conflict problems so far. The many marshlands make this an excellent spot for birdwatching.

General location: Dunbarton (7 miles southwest of Concord on NH 13)

Elevation change: The trails follow undulating terrain, with some short climbs.

Season: Late spring through fall. (ATVs are prohibited before May 23, due to muddy conditions.)

Services: Food is available at the Dunbarton Country Store just before the trailhead. Other services are available in Concord.

Hazards: Watch and listen for approaching ATVs and motorcycles. Be prepared to ride through some areas with soft, sandy surfaces.

Rescue index: You will be up to 2 miles from traveled roads.

Land status: State-maintained trails on federal land

Maps: A brochure with small maps of this and five other multiuse trails is available from the New Hampshire Division of Parks and Recreation, Bureau of Trails. A trail map is also posted at the parking area. Also see Hopkinton and Weare quadrangles, USGS 7.5 minute series.

Finding the trail: From Concord, take NH 13 south. At Pages Corner, turn left to continue on NH 13. A mile beyond and immediately after the Dunbarton Country Store, turn right onto Winslow Road. Follow the signs to "OHRV Parking."

RIDE 20 · Hopkinton-Everett Lake Project

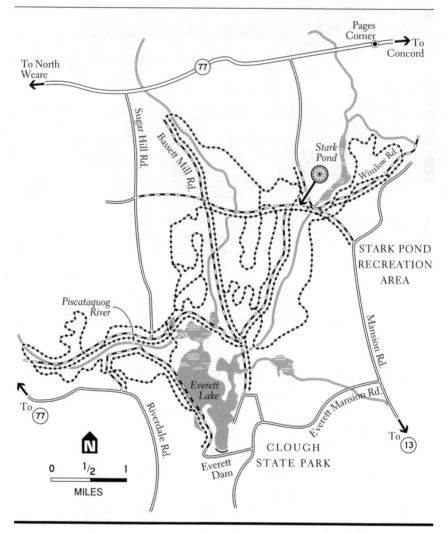

Source of additional information:

New Hampshire Division of Parks and Recreation, Trails Bureau
P.O. Box 1856
172 Pembroke Road
Concord, NH 03302-1856
(603) 271-3254

Notes on the trail: Several trails fan out from the parking area. Trail junctions are marked, and they are keyed to the Bureau of Trails' map. The easiest riding can be found on the dirt roads to the south of the parking area.

RIDE 21 · Bear Brook State Park

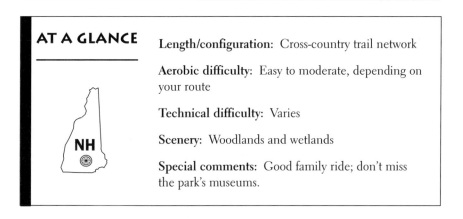

AT A GLANCE

Length/configuration: Cross-country trail network

Aerobic difficulty: Easy to moderate, depending on your route

Technical difficulty: Varies

Scenery: Woodlands and wetlands

Special comments: Good family ride; don't miss the park's museums.

Located just a few miles from Concord, Bear Brook is one of New Hampshire's most popular mountain biking spots. This 9,500-acre park features 40 miles of trails, ranging from easy woods roads to narrower, more rugged trails in the southwestern portion of the park. Elsewhere in the park, you can fish, swim, and camp out.

The park also features two unique museums on its grounds. The Museum of Family Camping displays an impressive collection of camping artifacts: tents, stoves, packs of all descriptions, vintage Coleman lanterns, and even an early travel trailer. The New Hampshire Snowmobile Museum preserves the heritage of the state's pioneering efforts in over-the-snow transportation. In addition to a large collection of early snowmobiles of various makes, the museum's collection features a Model T Ford on skis and tracks instead of wheels, and a rare Lombard Log Hauler. Both museums are open daily from Memorial Day to Columbus Day.

General location: Allenstown

Elevation change: Some short climbs, no major hills

Season: Spring through early fall

Services: Water and camping are available on-site. Other services can be found in Concord.

Hazards: Watch out for hikers and other trail users.

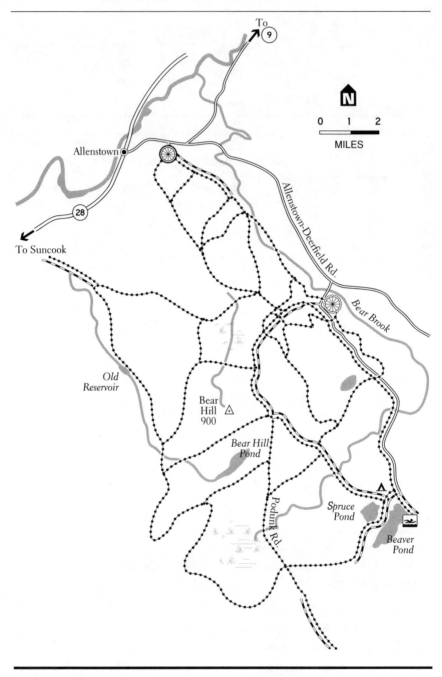

Rescue index: Some trails will take you up to 5 miles from the ranger station.

Land status: State park

Maps: A trail map is available at the park headquarters.

Finding the trail: From Concord, take US 3 south to Suncook. Turn left onto NH 28, and follow it for 3 miles. At Allenstown, turn right onto Deerfield Road and follow the signs for Bear Brook State Park to the parking area.

Sources of additional information:

Bear Brook State Park
RR 1, Box 507
Allenstown, NH 03275
(603) 485-9874

New Hampshire Division of Parks and Recreation, Parks Bureau
P.O. Box 1856
172 Pembroke Road
Concord, NH 03302-1856
(603) 271-3556

Museum of Family Camping
100 Athol Road
Richmond, NH 03470
(603) 239-4768

New Hampshire Snowmobile Association
P.O. Box 1856
Concord, NH 03302

Notes on the trail: Most of the trails are marked and numbered, but it might be helpful to bring along a compass. If you're feeling particularly ambitious, a lap around the park's perimeter trail will yield a 20-mile ride.

RIDE 22 · I-89 Bike Path

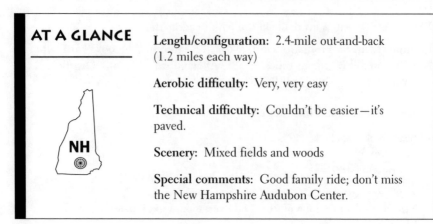

AT A GLANCE

Length/configuration: 2.4-mile out-and-back (1.2 miles each way)

Aerobic difficulty: Very, very easy

Technical difficulty: Couldn't be easier—it's paved.

Scenery: Mixed fields and woods

Special comments: Good family ride; don't miss the New Hampshire Audubon Center.

"You've got to be kidding," snorted my editor when he saw this ride. "A short, paved bike path in the suburbs? This is supposed to be a *mountain biking* book, remember?"

"I know, I know—so it isn't Crawford Notch. This path has some great things going for it, though."

"Such as?"

"For starters, it's just outside the city of Concord, so it's convenient for anyone visiting the state capitol. It's beyond the developed areas, and the meadows and woods along the trail are quite pretty."

"I'm sure the interstate highway is lovely, too," he said, rolling his eyes.

"Well, the highway construction *did* make this path possible, and the project included a separate bridge over Turkey Pond with a great view. Folks who ride on a cool morning can see the mist rising off the water, the waterfowl chasing breakfast . . ."

"Not enough," he said, cutting me short. "It needs something unique, like—"

"Like birdwatching?" I asked. He arched his eyebrows. I continued, "The New Hampshire Audubon Center sits a few hundred feet away from the trailhead. The center has educational exhibits, a simulated ecosystem, and a gift shop that sells all kinds of birdwatching essentials. Two hiking trails take you out to prime birdwatching locations around Turkey Pond. It's a great place to take kids before or after the ride. Trust me—they'll *love* it!"

"Okay," he said.

General location: Southwest of Concord

Elevation change: Not much, just some modest rolls in the terrain

Season: Spring through fall

Services: Restaurants, groceries, and lodging can be found in the Concord area.

RIDE 22 · I-89 Bike Path

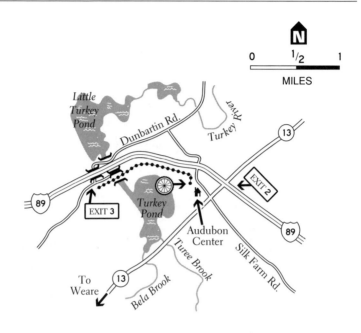

Hazards: Watch for the occasional jogger or dog-walker.

Rescue index: Civilization is always close at hand.

Land status: State-maintained trail

Maps: None necessary

Finding the trail: From Exit 2 of Interstate 89, take NH 13 toward Weare. The intersection with Silk Farm Road is just a few hundred feet away from the interstate; turn right. A sign marking the trailhead is a quarter of a mile ahead on the left. Park along the side of the road or at the New Hampshire Audubon Center (just before the trailhead, on the left) and stop in for a visit before or after your ride.

Sources of additional information:

New Hampshire Audubon Center
Silk Farm Road
Concord, NH 03301

Banagan's Cycling Company
27 South Main Street
Concord, NH 03301
(603) 225-3330

So it isn't Crawford Notch—at least there's good bird-watching along the way.

Notes on the trail: The trail is paved all the way, which makes for fast riding, but why rush it? Keep it in a low gear and savor the flora and fauna. The trail ends at a paved access road, which is good for another 1,000 feet of riding before you reach a main road. When you get there, turn around and enjoy the ride back.

WINNIPESAUKEE
(LAKES COUNTRY)

This is New Hampshire's summer resort country. There are moments in the height of summer when it seems like half of urban New England—the half that owns boats instead of hiking boots—is here on vacation. Like Henry Fonda and Katharine Hepburn in the movie *On Golden Pond* (which was filmed here), people come to go boating in the daytime, watch the sunset from screened-in porches, and be smiled upon by the Great Spirit.

Lakes Country serves as a kind of transitional zone between the flatlands of southern New Hampshire and the White Mountains. Lake Winnipesaukee is the big lake in the region, at 45,500 acres, but there are many others: Ossipee, Squam and Little Squam, Winnisquam, Wentworth, and a host of smaller ones. The land between the lakes is filled with interesting nooks and crannies that provide good riding.

Eric Stinson's *Mountain Biking and Hiking the Belknap Range of Lake Winnipesaukee* provides details on trails near Laconia, the largest town in Lakes Country. It's a local, self-published guidebook, and copies are hard to come by (Eric's day job keeps him quite busy these days). Try the Sundial Shop in downtown Laconia, or Pinces Sport Shop, a bicycle shop just east of town on NH 11A.

Suggested Reading: *Blue Highways* by William Least Heat Moon. Very little of Heat Moon's 13,000-mile journey across America actually took place in New Hampshire, of course, but he made an extended stop in Lakes Country and met with some classic Granite State folk here. If you like travel writing, and somehow haven't happened into this one yet, now's as good a time as any to read it.

RIDE 23 · Blue Job Mountain

AT A GLANCE

NH

Length/configuration: 8.5-mile loop

Aerobic difficulty: Moderate climbing

Technical difficulty: Some rugged double-track

Scenery: Woods and fields

Special comments: A pleasant ride in the country.

Portions of Lakes Country have, like any popular vacation area, succumbed to Tourist Trap Syndrome, a nasty infection of gift shops, mini-golf courses, and garish theme restaurants. Sure, these blighted areas hold a certain fascination for visiting cyclists (where else are you going to get a good latte?), but it's tough to find good off-road riding there. Mountain biking demands sacrifice. Turn away from the neon! Look to the hills!

This ride gets you away from the hubbub and onto some good back roads in the neighborhood of Blue Job Mountain State Forest (and Rochester's municipal drinking-water supply). New Hampshire isn't exactly famous for good farmland, but it does actually have some, and you'll see it along the way, too. If you're eager for more after finishing the loop, try exploring the numerous other dirt roads to the west and south (Barn Door Gap, Evans Mountain, and Parker Mountain are nearby spots to look for more riding).

General location: Farmington (6 miles west of Rochester)

Elevation change: About 400 feet of elevation gain

Season: Late spring through fall

Services: All services are available in Rochester.

Hazards: Watch for light traffic on traveled roads.

Rescue index: You are within a mile of traveled roads or inhabited areas at all times.

Land status: Public roads

Maps: Page 37 of DeLorme's *New Hampshire Atlas and Gazetteer*. Also see Baxter Lake quadrangle, USGS 7.5 minute series.

Finding the trail: From Rochester, take NH 202A about 2 miles to Meaderboro Corner and turn right onto Meaderboro Road. Drive for about 3 miles. At the intersection with Cross Road (where the road surface becomes dirt), continue straight and park along the wide, secluded portion of road just beyond.

RIDE 23 · Blue Job Mountain

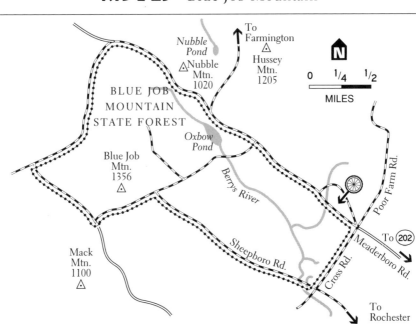

Source of additional information:

Wheel Power
183 Water Street
Exeter, NH 03833
(603) 772-6343

Notes on the trail: From your parking spot, ride back to the intersection and turn right onto Cross Road. You'll soon see a reservoir on your right; just after it, turn right onto a four-wheel-drive road (Sheepboro Road). When you reach the first **T** intersection, turn left. Climb along the slope of Blue Job Mountain and turn right at the next **T** intersection, to follow the dirt road. A third **T** intersection is about 0.7 mile beyond; turn right again. This unmaintained dirt road carries you through a conservation easement on the other side of Blue Job, and down to Meaderboro Road. Turn right and continue straight for the remainder of the ride to return to the starting point.

RIDE 24 · Liberty Hill

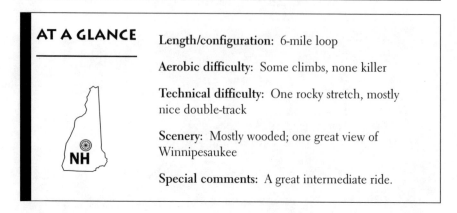

AT A GLANCE

Length/configuration: 6-mile loop

Aerobic difficulty: Some climbs, none killer

Technical difficulty: One rocky stretch, mostly nice double-track

Scenery: Mostly wooded; one great view of Winnipesaukee

NH

Special comments: A great intermediate ride.

The Presidential Range it ain't, but the Belknap Range is a pretty cool place to ride. Tucked in among the 2,000-foot peaks are a variety of trails, mostly intended for winter use, but suitable for biking, too. Hang out at one of Laconia's bike shops or a snowmobile dealership, and you'll get tips on some worthwhile trails to explore. If you're in a hurry to start riding, though, this is the ride to do first.

Laconia's hard-core mountain bikers call this loop through the Belknaps a "training" ride (in other words, it doesn't slow them down much). It mostly follows double-track trails that see frequent use by snowmobilers in wintertime and winds through dense forest. An excellent view of the lake and the Belknap Range hits you early in the ride. The trailhead is convenient to Laconia, too.

General location: 3 miles east of Laconia

Elevation change: A lot of ups and downs throughout the ride, adding up to less than 600 feet of gain

Season: Late spring through fall

Services: All services can be found in Laconia.

Hazards: One heavily eroded climb; mudholes and windfall in places

Rescue index: You're within 2 miles of inhabited areas at all times.

Land status: Class VI roads and snowmobile trails

Maps: Page 36 of DeLorme's *New Hampshire Atlas and Gazetteer*. Also see Laconia quadrangle, USGS 7.5 minute series.

Finding the trail: From NH 11A east, take the first right turn after the US 3 underpass, then a left turn onto Liberty Hill Road. Bear right onto Wild Acres Road; watch for the radio tower on your left. Park by the tower (keep to the edge of the turnaround: it's used by school buses that serve the children's camp a quarter of a mile beyond).

Source of additional information: *Mountain Biking and Hiking the Belknap*

RIDE 24 • Liberty Hill

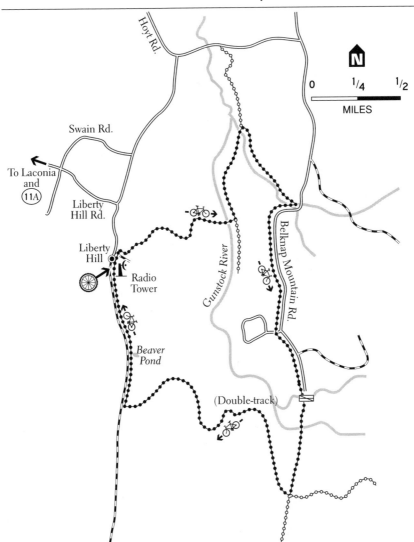

Range of Lake Winnipesaukee, a booklet by local mountain biker Eric Stinson, provides details of this and other rides.

Notes on the trail: From the tower, a side road heads into the woods for a short way. Take it for 100 feet or so, and watch for a trail on your left. Take it through the trees and into a large meadow. If you find yourself enjoying the view, you're on your way!

Lake Winnipesaukee and the Belknaps arrayed majestically before you.

The trail drops into the woods and zigzags to a jeep trail at the bottom. Turn left and take it for a half mile. Just past the creek, turn right onto a sandy trail, which follows the creek to a paved road. At the pavement, turn right, ride for 0.8 mile, and turn left at the **T** intersection. The pavement ends at a gate; continue on the Class VI road beyond. The uphill portion of this road is heavily eroded and may reduce you to walking (only for a half mile or so). At the end of the climb, watch for an intersecting trail and turn right (you'll see a large boulder placed in the middle of this trail).

This trail twists through the forest in a generally westerly direction. A few trails branch off—stay on the main one by following the four-wheel-drive tracks and the snowmobile blazes. Eventually you'll reach a **T** intersection; turn right to follow snowmobile trail "15N," pass a beaver pond, climb one last hill, and you're back at the radio tower.

RIDE 25 · Belknap Saddle

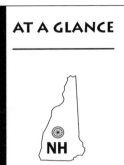

AT A GLANCE

NH

Length/configuration: 2-mile loop

Aerobic difficulty: Tough climb up

Technical difficulty: Tough ride down

Scenery: Forest, meadow, blueberries

Special comments: This trail is suitable for an ambitious intermediate cyclist.

It was a hot, muggy, buggy afternoon as I rode the gated portion of Belknap Mountain Road, following an old snowmobile map in search of some good mountain biking. What I'd ridden so far wasn't terribly exciting, and I was on the verge of calling it quits, when I happened upon a couple of mountain bikers on a water break. One of them was a local guy, Brian Heath, who spends much of his free time cranking through the Lakes Region.

He and a friend from Florida were taking a grand tour of the Belknaps and invited me to join them. Brian looked like a hard-core rider, and he was riding a fully suspended rig; there was no way I could keep up. Instead, we rode this short loop together, and then they continued on their way. This is a pretty demanding ride, but it's short enough that moderately skilled riders can hang in there—especially during wild blueberry season.

General location: 3 miles south of Gilford

Elevation change: From pavement to meadow is a 400-foot climb.

Season: Late spring through fall

Services: All services can be found in Laconia.

Hazards: Rough trail surface through most of the ride, and a steep, twisting, single-track descent

Rescue index: Inhabited areas are 2–3 miles away.

Land status: Class VI road and trails

Maps: Page 36 of DeLorme's *New Hampshire Atlas and Gazetteer*

Finding the trail: From Gilford, follow Belknap Mountain Road south to the end. Park on the shoulder near the gate.

Source of additional information: The aforementioned "grand tour" can be found in Eric Stinson's *Mountain Biking and Hiking the Belknap Range of Lake Winnipesaukee.* The grand tour of the Belknap Range *is* an all-day ride encompassing more than 20 miles and several mountain peaks.

RIDE 25 · Belknap Saddle

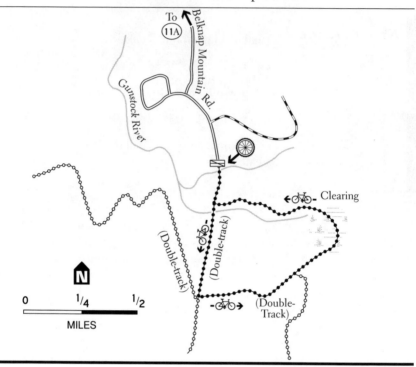

Notes on the trail: Take the unpaved road past the gate and into the woods. The uphill portion is rocky and very eroded; as it levels off, you'll reach a four-way junction of trails. Up to now, this ride has coincided with a portion of the Liberty Hill ride (see Ride 24); to continue on Belknap Saddle, you turn left here. The trail is blazed for snowmobiles; after about 0.4 mile of climbing, it forks. Bear left (the right fork continues to the top of Whiteface Mountain) and make your way up a steep but short run to the saddle.

The clearing here has wild blueberries (if you missed berry season, there are large rocks to relax on). Rest up, then head for the northwest edge of the clearing to find the trail for the descent. The ride down is narrow, twisting, rough, and never boring. At the bottom, turn right. The gate is just a few hundred feet ahead.

RIDE 26 · Hidden Valley

AT A GLANCE

Length/configuration: 6-mile out-and-back (3 miles each way)

Aerobic difficulty: Steady climbing

Technical difficulty: Very technical if you opt for the "scenic route"

Scenery: Wooded mountainside with overlooks to the valley below

Special comments: Other rides for various skill levels are available.

NH

Last time I'd set foot in a Boy Scout camp, I was still one myself. (Five years and only a First Class badge to show for it, but what fun!) I'd come to Hidden Valley Boy Scout Reservation to investigate the rumor that non-Scouts could bike here, and I arrived just in time for Reveille. Seeing all those teenage boys gathered 'round the flagpole, saluting with three fingers instead of just one like they do in my neighborhood, sure brought back the memories. Suddenly, I wanted to play Uno by the light of a Coleman lantern while sipping lumpy hot cocoa. I wanted to put a one-gallon milk jug on a stick and melt it over the campfire. I wanted to send some Tenderfoot off in search of a left-handed smoke shifter.

But I digress. Yes, the camp's program director assured me, mountain bikers are welcome here. The camp is full of Scouts throughout the summer and on most fall weekends, so a pedestrian-friendly riding style is called for. The ranger also asks that you check in at the administration building upon your arrival. Those caveats noted, grab your Trustworthy Loyal Helpful Friendly mountain bike and follow the trail to Round Pond.

General location: Gilmanton Iron Works (about 14 miles southeast of Laconia on NH 140)

Elevation change: You'll climb about 900 feet along the way.

Season: Late spring through fall

Services: Services can be found in Alton, 5 miles to the west, or Laconia.

Hazards: As noted above, watch for pedestrians, especially during the summer and on weekends.

Rescue index: The farther reaches of this ride take you a couple of miles from inhabited areas.

Land status: Privately owned by the Daniel Webster Council of the Boy Scouts of America

RIDE 26 · Hidden Valley

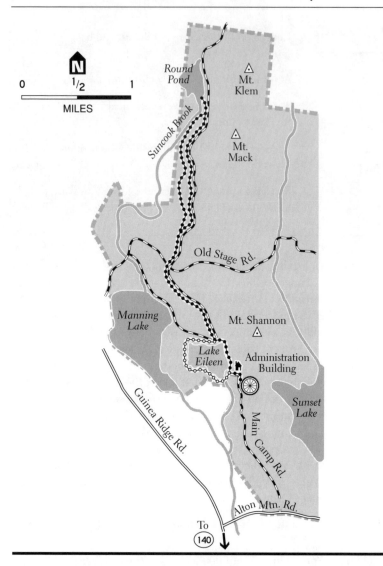

Maps: When you check in with the ranger at the administration building, ask for a copy of the reservation's trail map.

Finding the trail: The reservation is 4 miles north of Gilmanton Iron Works. Just west of town on NH 140, turn north onto Guinea Ridge Road and follow it past Crystal Lake. Turn right on Alton Mountain Road, then left onto the main camp road. Watch for the "Hidden Valley" signs at all intersections. The administration building is located by Lake Eileen.

The scenic route is worth the extra walking.

Source of additional information:

Hidden Valley Scout Reservation
RFD 1
P.O. Box 623
Gilmanton Iron Works, NH 03837
(603) 364-2900

Notes on the trail: From the administration building, take the access road around Lake Eileen. Several roads and trails branch off into the woods; the road to Round Pond, also known as the "red" trail, is marked with a New Hampshire Snowmobile Trail sign (or ask a nearby Scout).

After crossing the old stage road, the climb begins in earnest. At about 1.5 miles from headquarters, you'll be faced with a choice of two parallel routes: "via scenic vista and gorge" and "via truck road." If you take the scenic trail into the woods, prepare for *a lot* of walking and carrying, some spectacular views of the wooded valley, and, if the season is right (around mid-July), wild blueberries. The trail rejoins the road just before Round Pond; a marked side trail will take you to its shore. Once you're rested up, turn around and take the truck road back down the hill. Watch for waterbars, and keep your speed under control.

Some local riders continue past Round Pond and ride down the other side of the mountain to Gunstock (see Ride 27). For details on taking an extended ride all the way over the mountain, inquire at Gunstock.

Final Fascinatin' Fact: The 1959 edition of the *Boy Scout Handbook* features advertisements for 26-inch bicycle tires on *both* inside covers (and an ad for Bendix hubs opposite "L" in the index).

RIDE 27 · Gunstock

AT A GLANCE	**Configuration:** Cross-country trail network
	Aerobic difficulty: From easy to advanced
	Technical difficulty: From easy to moderate
NH	**Scenery:** Mostly wooded trails
	Special comments: Lots of good riding for novices; something for everyone.

Gunstock is a county-owned ski facility with a good cross-country trail net-work; it just might be the best-kept secret of the Belknap Range. Gunstock stacks up quite well against other cross-country resorts in New Hampshire: the terrain is varied and challenging, and trail maintenance is good. The new edition of their trail map, while somewhat crude, does have color-coding and land contours, and is keyed pretty well to the existing ski-trail signage. The staff knows their stuff, too. Thoughtfully placed, ultraconcise signage will call your attention to various scenic features ("Dam," for example) along the way.

General location: Gilford

Elevation change: As much as 1,300 feet of elevation gain, depending on the trails you ride

Season: Open daily 8 a.m.–6 p.m., Memorial Day weekend to Labor Day week-end; weekends only to Columbus Day weekend. Trail fee (in 1997): $4, all day (free to campground patrons, children age 5 and under, and seniors).

Services: Bike rentals and repairs, food, water, and camping are available on-site. Other services are available in Laconia.

Hazards: Some trails are shared with hikers and equestrians; use caution and yield when necessary.

Rescue index: Some trails take you 2–3 miles from assistance.

Land status: County-owned ski center

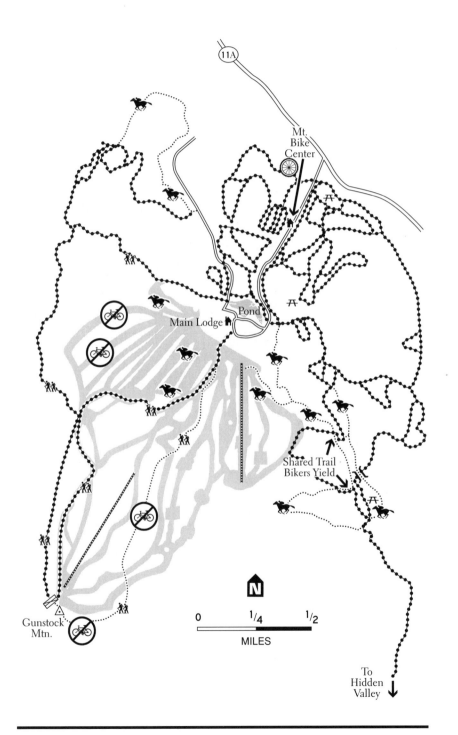

11A

Mt.
Bike
Center

Pond
Main Lodge

Shared Trail
Bikers Yield

Gunstock
Mtn.

N

0   1/4   1/2
MILES

To
Hidden
Valley

Ultraconcise interpretive
signage has been
provided by
the management.

Maps: A color map with contours is provided with the trail fee.

Finding the trail: The entrance to Gunstock is on NH 11A, 3 miles east of Gilford, and is prominently marked.

Source of additional information:

Gunstock
Route 11A
Gilford, NH 03246
(800) GUNSTOCK

RIDE 28 · Chamberlain-Reynolds Memorial Forest

AT A GLANCE

Length/configuration: 4-mile out-and-back (2 miles each way)

Aerobic difficulty: Mildly undulating lakeside trails

Technical difficulty: Mix of easy and intermediate

Scenery: Lakeside forest

Special comments: Find out why this pond is Golden.

Long before Hollywood came here to film *On Golden Pond*, Squam Lake was regarded as a special place. The lake is one of the most pristine in New England, and local residents fight hard to keep it that way. Their organization, the Squam Lakes Association, works to keep water quality high, shorefront development low, and powerboating under control. They also manage the public lands along the lake, including this 159-acre tract of forest.

The riding here varies from easy woods roads to gnarly narrow trails, and the forest is small enough that anyone can slog through the tricky parts and not have to worry about stranding themselves in the wilderness. This ride makes a great accompaniment to a day of nonbiking activities in one of America's premier vacation spots.

General location: Holderness

Elevation change: Minor undulations in terrain; no significant climbing

Season: Late spring through fall

Services: Food and lodging can be found in Holderness, 4 miles north on US 3, or Meredith, 4 miles south on US 3. All services can be found in Ashland, 7 miles north on US 3.

Hazards: Watch for hikers and the occasional muddy spot. Some trails elsewhere in the forest have rocks or heavy undergrowth.

Rescue index: The area surrounding the forest boundaries is inhabited.

Land status: Forest owned by the New England Forestry Foundation and managed for public use

Maps: Sometimes available at trailhead. Also see "A Primer for Squam," a pamphlet published by the Squam Lakes Association.

Finding the trail: From Holderness, take US 3 east 3.5 miles and turn left on College Road. A small, clearly marked parking area is about 0.5 mile ahead on the left.

RIDE 28 · Chamberlain-Reynolds Memorial Forest

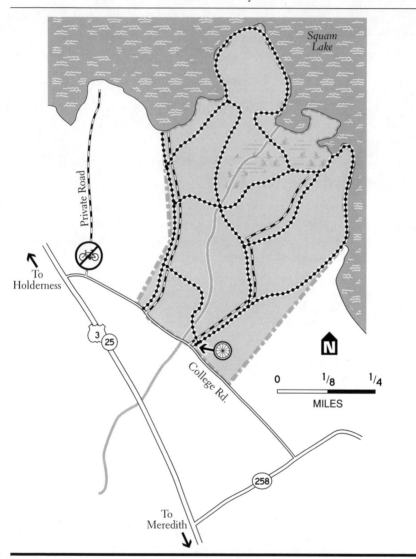

Source of additional information:

Squam Lakes Association
P.O. Box 204
Holderness, NH 03245
(603) 968-7336
The SLA sells a trail guide and a color topographic map of the area,
which may be useful in locating additional riding.

A lovely spot on the
shore of "Golden Pond."

Notes on the trail: From the parking area, backtrack a few hundred feet west
along College Road to the first dirt road on the right. Take this road, which hugs
the forest's western boundary, straight to the shore.

Other trails vary in suitability for mountain biking (feel free to explore them
if you don't mind some walking and carrying). Don't worry about getting lost; it's
a small park, and you'll find signs at most trail junctions.

RIDE 29 · Russel C. Chase Bridge-Falls Path

AT A GLANCE
————————

NH

Length/configuration: 2.4-mile out-and-back (1.2 miles each way)

Aerobic difficulty: Easy; almost perfectly level

Technical difficulty: Smooth, packed-gravel surface

Scenery: Village edge and lakeshore

Special comments: Great family ride; don't miss the Wright Museum.

Here it is, Mom and Dad: this might *look* like an ordinary rail trail, but it's got a secret surprise that will amaze your kids! Want to turn their day into an educational experience before they realize it? It's easy! Park at the Wolfeborough depot, get the bikes off the roof, and hit the trail. Watch for the bridge at Wolfeboro Falls, about a half mile up, and as you're crossing it, point off to your right and exclaim, "Look everyone! There's a tank crashing through that building over there!!!"

Once you've got them jumping up and down for a closer look, cross Route 28 (looking both ways for traffic, of course), and step up to the Wright Museum of American Enterprise. The Wright Museum (not Wilbur, Orville, or Frank Lloyd, by the way, but E. Stanley, a veteran of the U. S. Marine Corps) has great exhibits relating to life on the "home front" during World War II, and a hall full of military vehicles of the same era. They'll learn what Boy Scouts collected tires for, why the Army bought cameras from amateur photographers, and what a Norden bombsight (like the one used over Hiroshima) looks like.

Now, revel in the satisfaction of knowing that you're a really cool parent.

General location: Wolfeboro

Elevation change: Negligible

Season: Mid-spring through fall

Services: All services can be found in Wolfeboro.

Hazards: Watch for traffic at the NH 28 grade crossing.

Rescue index: Civilization is always close at hand.

Land status: State-owned railroad bed

Maps: None necessary. (The Wolfeboro Chamber of Commerce publishes a free map of the village that might be handy, though.)

Finding the trail: Park near the depot on Railroad Avenue, one block north of Main Street.

RIDE 29 · Russel C. Chase Bridge-Falls Path

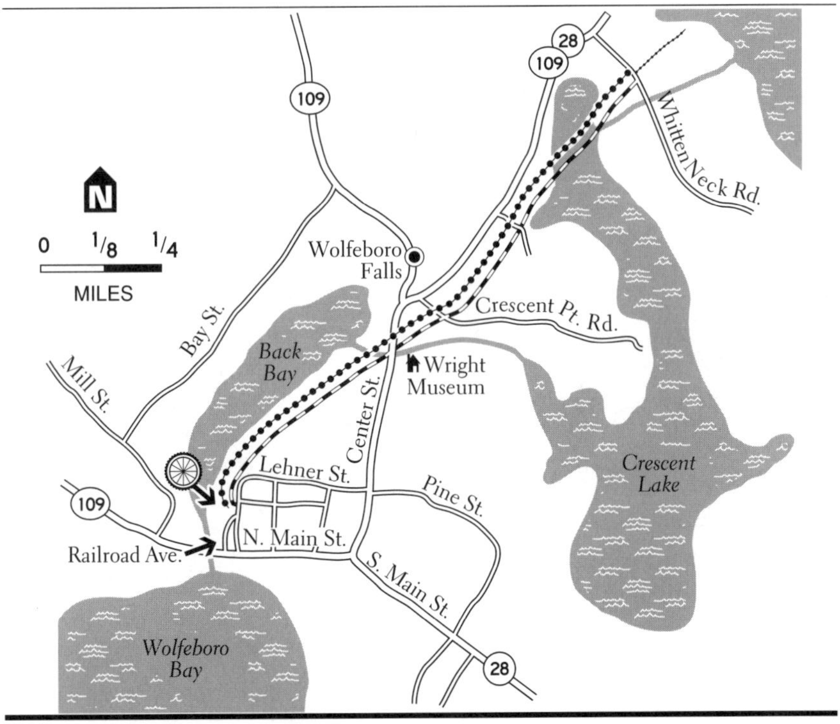

Sources of additional information:

Nordic Skier Sports
Box 269
North Main Street
Wolfeboro, NH 03894
(603) 569-3151
Nordic Skier serves the area's mountain bikers and publishes
a map and guide for more advanced local rides.

The Wright Museum of American Enterprise
77 Center Street
Wolfeboro, NH 03894
(603) 569-1212

Notes on the trail: From Wolfeborough depot, take the trail north. The portion
to Wolfeboro Falls is broad, well maintained, and even has streetlights and park
benches along the way. North of the museum and NH 28, the trail is a somewhat rougher dirt one, between or beside existing rails. For several hundred feet
it takes an embankment across the end of Crescent Lake. At the moment, the
trail has been graded only three-quarters of a mile past NH 28, but the state plans

As you approach the bridge at Wolfboro Falls, watch for the building (to your right) with the World War II tank crashing through it.

to develop the right-of-way for several more miles. When you see weeds where the trail ought to be, turn around immediately and return to the depot. Finish the day with a visit to the ice cream shop across the street from the depot (they make their own, and the Molasses Gingersnap is *really* good).

PEMIGEWASSET
(THE PLYMOUTH-LINCOLN AREA)

The White Mountains might look like just a bunch of peaks to you and me, but geographers divide them up into four distinct ranges: the Sandwich Range, the Franconia Range, the Presidentials (of which Mount Washington is by far the most famous), and Carter-Moriah (in the northeast corner, around Gorham). This section explores the first two, in the southern and eastern section of the White Mountain National Forest. These ranges are the easiest to access from the flatlands: just hop onto Interstate 93 and take any exit numbered 24 or above.

Approach the White Mountains from the south, and the demarcation is clear and startling. The foothills to the southwest are nowhere near as rugged as the White Mountains themselves, and the broad valley of the Connecticut River appears to be a remote extension of the flat coastal region. No matter how flat or lumpy you like your mountain bike trails, you can find one to your liking in this area.

Plymouth, the gateway to this side of the White Mountains, is home to Plymouth State College and all the accouterments you'd expect in a college town: pizza joints, watering holes, bookstores, and (of course) a good bike shop. Villages farther north—Campton, Waterville Valley, North Woodstock, Lincoln, and Franconia—are all to some degree or another dependent on tourism: hikers and campers in summertime, leaf peepers in the fall, and skiers in the winter. East from Lincoln runs the Kancamagus Highway, a scenic road constructed in the 1930s with forest visitors foremost in mind (not that existing roads weren't scenic enough!). If you overlook the fact that virtually all of the White Mountain National Forest is second-growth woods (the loggers came and went decades ago), you're surrounded by otherwise pristine wilderness wherever you go.

Suggested Reading: *Mapping the White Mountains* by John T. B. Mudge. Appropriately printed on a single large sheet like a map, this book depicts the cartographer's art from the earliest days of the New World explorers all the way up to recent work by Bradford Washburn and the Appalachian Mountain Club. Reproduced in full is the hilarious 1871 edition of Leavitt's Map of the White

Mountains, a souvenir map with engravings of not one, not two, but *three* Courageous Pioneers in the Act of Killing Bears. Also, *The Great Stone Face* by Nathaniel Hawthorne is a short story featuring that most famous of New Hampshire landmarks. If *The House of the Seven Gables* put you to sleep in high school English, here's your chance to make up for it.

RIDE 30 · Plymouth Mountain

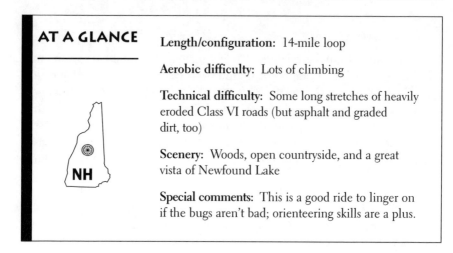

AT A GLANCE

Length/configuration: 14-mile loop

Aerobic difficulty: Lots of climbing

Technical difficulty: Some long stretches of heavily eroded Class VI roads (but asphalt and graded dirt, too)

Scenery: Woods, open countryside, and a great vista of Newfound Lake

Special comments: This is a good ride to linger on if the bugs aren't bad; orienteering skills are a plus.

"Sure, it's an intermediate ride," Tim Gotwols, proprietor of Riverside Cycles, told me. But seven miles into it, I wasn't so certain. The Class VI was smooth and grassy, but it kept going up, and up, and up. The deer flies were biting, too. I gave myself another coat of DEET and continued pushing the bike up a slope that never seemed to end.

But it did, and at the top, surrounded by woods, lay a tiny cemetery. Maybe two dozen brittle, eroded headstones lay about, none dated past the 1830s. A faded little American flag, with a Revolutionary War medallion on its stick, stood next to one stone. While I couldn't read the names, I could follow the story. These were the original settlers of Hebron township, the builders of the forlorn stone fences along the road. Their grandchildren went off to fight the Civil War, discovered western states where dirt was more plentiful than rocks, and left their sidehill New Hampshire farms for the trees to reclaim. Only the fences and gravestones are left, and the gravestones aren't weathering well.

Reluctantly, I remounted and started down the other side of the mountain. Not every good ride is an easy one.

General location: Plymouth

RIDE 30 · Plymouth Mountain

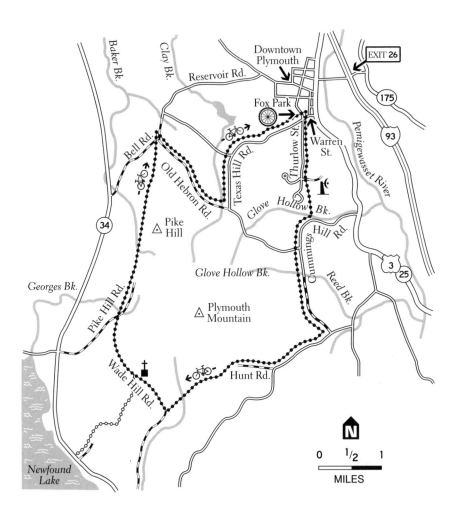

Elevation change: About 2,300 feet of altitude gain in total, most of it in the first half of the ride

Season: Early summer through fall

Services: All services can be found in Plymouth.

Hazards: Heavy erosion in spots

Rescue index: Along the eastern part of the loop, you will be up to 2 miles from inhabited areas.

Newfound Lake lies below; a pioneer cemetery lies beyond.

Land status: Active and abandoned public roads

Maps: Ashland quadrangle, USGS 7.5 minute series

Finding the trail: From US 3 at the south edge of Plymouth, turn west onto Warren Street. Park at Fox Park, 3 blocks ahead on the right.

Source of additional information:

Riverside Cycles
4 Riverside Drive
Ashland, NH 03217
(603) 968-9676
Proprietor Tim Gotwols is an authority on mountain biking in the Squam area and the southern White Mountains.

Notes on the trail: From Fox Park go back to the corner, turn right onto Thurlow Street, and ride to the top of the hill. Bear left onto the dirt road toward the radio tower and look immediately on the right for a trail into the woods. This Class VI road heads almost due south, steadily losing altitude, and is for the most part in pretty good shape. It ends at a bend in a paved road at the bottom of the hill; continue straight and upward.

At the next intersection, continue straight on a graded dirt road and enjoy a gentle descent. At the end, a right turn takes you uphill again. Ride for about a mile and turn right onto Hunt Road, which is graded dirt. Keep climbing. Hunt Road dwindles to Class VI near the top of the climb, and ducks into the woods. Continue straight (don't take the logging road you'll see on your right). The road here is rustic but not extremely technical.

When you emerge from the woods, you'll see a barn and farmhouse and, off in the distance, Newfound Lake. At this point, you've traveled about six miles and are now about 1,200 feet above sea level. The grassy trail on your right, on this side of the barn, is the road that climbs (another 360 feet of gain) up to the cemetery.

As I mentioned, it's a tough climb, but at least it's shady, and if you're lucky, the wild raspberries will be in. Catch your breath among the headstones, then continue straight (ignore the marked snowmobile trail on your left). The ride is grassy and gentle here; farther down it gets rockier. The trail ends at a graded dirt road with a house opposite. (Note to those of you navigating by the USGS Ashland quadrangle: this particular junction is at the very edge of the sheet, next to the 42 minute, 30 second tick.) This is Pike Hill Road. Turn right, climb, and stay straight as it becomes Class VI road again.

At this point, you've done most of the hard climbing, but the most technical riding lies just ahead. Over the next 2.5 miles, you'll climb about 200 feet, crest, and then lose about 600 feet. The road starts out grassy with some marshy spots, but as you descend, the road becomes more eroded, until it's a solid river of boulders. Those less technically oriented (or riding rigid forks) will probably walk most of this (I did). Eventually, you'll reach graded dirt again. Turn right onto Old Hebron Road. About 1.5 miles of riding brings you to Texas Hill Road; hang a left onto the asphalt and enjoy the 2-mile descent into town. (Don't enjoy it so much that you shoot past Fox Park on your left.)

RIDE 31 · Bridgewater Hill

AT A GLANCE	
	Length/configuration: 5-mile loop
	Aerobic difficulty: Plenty of climbing
	Technical difficulty: Rustic trails and eroded dirt roads
NH	**Scenery:** Deep woods
	Special comments: Orienteering skills are a plus.

This challenging loop takes a snowmobile trail up the side of Bridgewater Mountain and follows an abandoned town road back down. The trail gets a little faint in spots; for those of you with a good nose for trails, this is a good ride with which to impress a navigationally challenged friend. (Screw it up, though, and you'll never hear the end of it.)

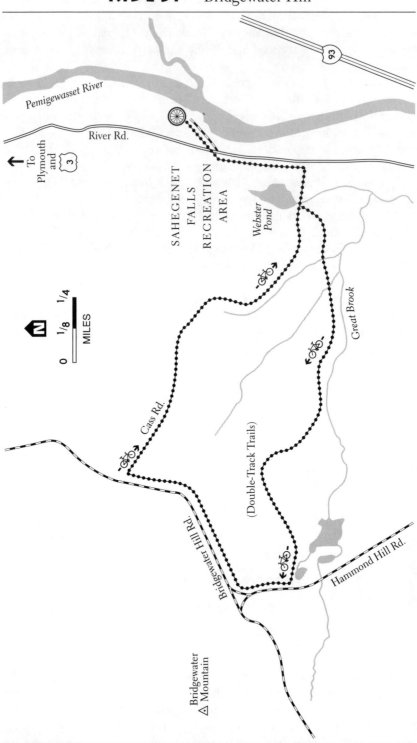

Pemigewasset River

93

River Rd.

To Plymouth and 3

SAHEGENET FALLS RECREATION AREA

Webster Pond

Great Brook

N

0 1/8 1/4
MILES

Cass Rd.

(Double-Track Trails)

Bridgewater Hill Rd.

Hammond Hill Rd.

Bridgewater △ Mountain

You could save almost 100 feet of vertical climb on this ride by parking on River Road instead of down by the river, but don't. Why not? As you work your way up and down the hill, trying to stay ahead of the bugs, look forward to dipping your toes in the Pemigewasset at ride's end. That should keep you going through many a surface hazard.

General location: West of Ashland

Elevation change: About 700 feet of altitude gain

Season: Early summer through fall

Services: All services can be found in Ashland, 4 miles east, or Plymouth, 5 miles north.

Hazards: Some parts of the trail are severely eroded; poor trail markings.

Rescue index: You will be up to 1.5 miles from assistance.

Land status: Snowmobile trail; active and abandoned public roads

Maps: Ashland quadrangle, USGS 7.5 minute series (invaluable for terrain information, but it doesn't show the snowmobile trail)

Finding the trail: From US 3 between Plymouth and Ashland, take River Road south to the Sahegenet Falls Recreation Area—it's on the left and clearly signed.

Source of additional information:

Riverside Cycles
4 Riverside Drive
Ashland, NH 03217
(603) 968-9676

Notes on the trail: From the recreation area, climb back up to River Road and turn left. After about 0.4 mile, turn right onto a Class VI road next to a barn. After a very short distance, you'll see Webster Pond through the trees on your right. On your left will be a snowmobile trail blazed with orange diamonds. Take it.

The trail parallels the nearby brook and starts climbing, getting progressively rougher. A big climb takes you to a stand of pines, where the trail gets faint and the blazes disappear. Follow the barbed-wire fence on your right until the blazes reappear. Follow the blazes until the trail ends at a graded dirt road and turn right.

A three-way junction of graded dirt roads is just ahead; bear right. Ride for about 0.6 mile and look closely for a Class VI road on your right, among the trees. It's easy to mistake it for a private driveway, but it has stone fences on both sides and runs straight for 1,000 feet or more. This road climbs gently for a while before the descent begins. The steepest portion is heavily eroded; beyond that, the descent is pretty easy. Ignore any side roads. At the bottom, you'll see Webster Pond again, this time on your left. Ride out to the road and retrace the route to your parking spot.

RIDE 32 · Orange Cove Trail

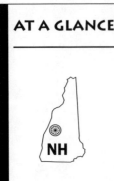

AT A GLANCE

Length/configuration: 5-mile out-and-back (2.5 miles each way)

Aerobic difficulty: Moderate amount of climbing

Technical difficulty: Double-track with some erosion

Scenery: Panoramic views of Mount Cardigan

Special comments: There is an optional extension to Sculptured Rocks for advanced bushwhackers.

This short jaunt into the woods makes a good ride for those who are aerobically gifted but navigationally impaired. Once you've got the bike pointed toward the right trail, simply ride up to the top, turn around, and descend. Along the way, you'll parallel Number Seven Brook, pass a quiet pond, and catch some good views of nearby Mount Cardigan. If you care to extend your stay, hike the trail the rest of the way to Cardigan's summit (biking isn't recommended), or, if you're feeling particularly adventurous (and well prepared), see if you can ride onward to Sculptured Rocks Natural Area to the northeast.

General location: Orange (15 miles east of Lebanon on US 4)

Elevation change: There's about 500 feet of elevation gain on this ride.

Season: Late spring through fall

Services: Food, lodging, and camping can be found in Canaan (3 miles west) and along US 4. There are bike shops in Lebanon and Plymouth.

Hazards: Watch for moderate surface hazards throughout the ride.

Rescue index: Assistance will be up to 2 miles away.

Land status: An abandoned public road

Maps: Mount Cardigan quadrangle, USGS 7.5 minute series

Finding the trail: From US 4, turn north onto NH 118. Travel for a half mile and turn right onto Orange Road (follow the sign for Cardigan Mountain State Forest). About 2.5 miles beyond, you'll cross a bridge; immediately after it, turn left onto a paved road. After the last house on the left, there's a cable across the road. Find a spot along the shoulder to park.

RIDE 32 · Orange Cove Trail

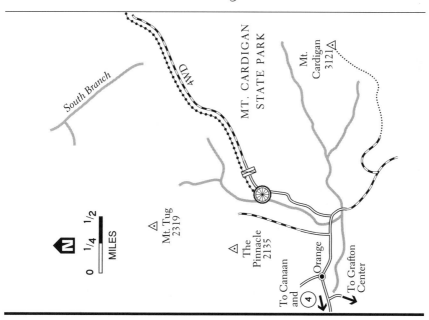

Source of additional information:

Greasey Wheel Bicycle Shop
40 South Main Street
Plymouth, NH 03264
(603) 536-3655
Mountain bikers meet here weekly for group rides.

Notes on the trail: From your parking spot, pass the cable (it's not intended to restrict cyclists) and head up the hill. The trail ends at the pond; turn around and enjoy the descent. (A more rugged trail extends northeast from the pond to Sculptured Rocks Natural Area, about 4 miles beyond. Local cyclists claim it's rough but ridable.)

RIDE 33 · Boston Lot Lake

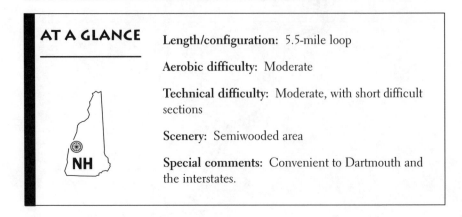

AT A GLANCE

Length/configuration: 5.5-mile loop

Aerobic difficulty: Moderate

Technical difficulty: Moderate, with short difficult sections

Scenery: Semiwooded area

Special comments: Convenient to Dartmouth and the interstates.

New Hampshire's outpost of the Ivy League is, of course, Dartmouth College in Hanover, located in the broad valley of the Connecticut River. Dartmouth was founded in 1769 by Reverend Eleazer Wheelock in an attempt (I'm paraphrasing the original mission statement here) to knock a little Christian sense into the savage youths of local Indian tribes. Happily, the institution has long since moved on to other educational activities.

With New Hampshire's most famous college nearby, you *knew* there had to be some good mountain biking around somewhere, right? Bingo. This ride up to Boston Lot Lake utilizes some conveniently placed utility roads for a biking experience guaranteed to rid your mind of stuffy academic thoughts. (If you're not suffering from any such thoughts at the moment, feel free to ride anyway.)

General location: Lebanon

Elevation change: About 300 feet of elevation gain, most of it on a short, steep climb to the lake

Season: Early summer through fall

Services: All services are available in Lebanon and Hanover.

Hazards: Watch for surface hazards on the trail around the lake. Use caution in descending from the lake to the highway. Watch for traffic on NH 10.

Rescue index: You are within a half mile of inhabited areas at all times.

Land status: Public roads and privately owned utility roads

Maps: Hanover quadrangle, USGS 7.5 minute series

Finding the trail: Take NH 10 to Gould Road (about 4 miles north of I-89) and follow it east to Sachem Village. Park along this road next to the field on your right.

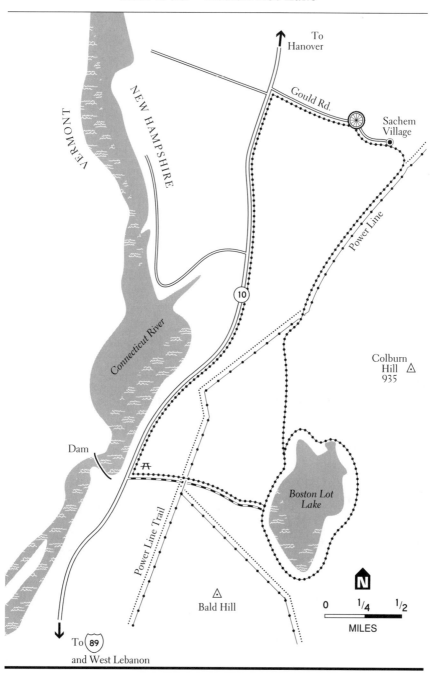

To
Hanover

Gould Rd.

Sachem
Village

NEW HAMPSHIRE

VERMONT

Power Line

Colburn
Hill
935

10

Connecticut River

Dam

Boston Lot
Lake

Power Line Trail

Bald Hill

N

0   1/4   1/2

MILES

To 89
and West Lebanon

Sources of additional information:

Tom Mowatt Cycles
213 Mechanic Street
Lebanon, NH 03766
(603) 448-5556

Omar & Bob's Sportshop
7 Allen Street
Hanover, NH 03755
(603) 643-3525

Notes on the trail: From your parking spot, go to the end of Gould Road and take a single-track trail east into the woods. Turn right onto the power-line trail and follow it for a little over a mile. Watch for a trail on your left (where the power line bears to the right), take it, and ride straight up the hill to the lake.

You can ride the trail around the lake in either direction; watch carefully for the white and blue blazes. A gravel road on the west side of the lake will take you down to NH 10 (where you'll find a picnic area). Turn right to head toward Gould Road.

RIDE 34 · Waterville Valley (Lift-serviced)

AT A GLANCE

Configuration: Lift-serviced trail network

Aerobic difficulty: Gravity does it for you.

Technical difficulty: Easy to fairly advanced

Scenery: Semiwooded

Special comments: Half the hill at a premium price!

NH

Waterville Valley has been in the lift-serviced mountain biking business longer than any other ski resort in New Hampshire. I wish I could say that they've got the most developed bike program to show for it. To be honest, they don't. The trails show more wear and tear than other downhill resorts. Trail signage is skimpy. The map comes off an office copier and isn't even up-to-date. All this for a lift-ticket price that's well above average. (On the plus side, their bike shop is really nice.)

RIDE 34 · Waterville Valley (Lift-serviced)

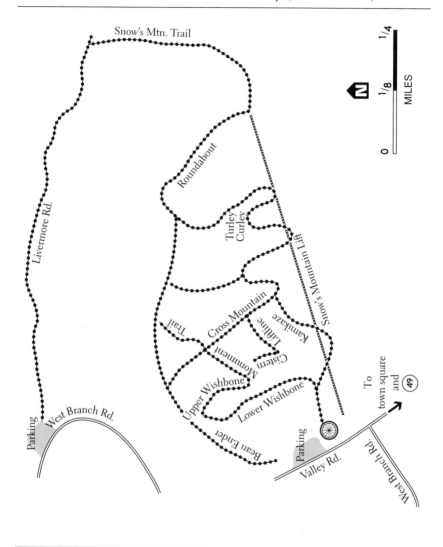

Snow's Mountain, a lower peak where the mountain bike chairlift operates, has 600 feet of drop. Although that's far lower than any other peak currently lifting bikes, it isn't necessarily a drawback. A beginning downhiller could feel comfortable here, and this is perhaps the only mountain where I'd take kids. (I even saw one man towing his child in a Burley trailer, something that would be illadvised at any other downhill spot.) But is it worth the price? Perhaps, if you like Waterville Valley's nonbiking amenities.

Genesee Mike, the author's daring steed, dangles by his rear wheel enroute to the peak of Snow's Mountain.

General location: Waterville Valley

Elevation change: 600 feet of vertical drop from the summit

Season: Open 10 a.m.–5 p.m. weekends, Memorial Day weekend to July 4; daily through Labor Day weekend; weekends through Columbus Day weekend. Rates (in 1997): $10, single ride; $20, all day (reduced rates for children and seniors).

Services: Bike rentals and repairs are available on-site. All services are available in town.

Hazards: Keep your speed under control.

Rescue index: You are generally within a mile of assistance.

Land status: Privately operated ski resort on U.S. Forest Service land

Maps: A black-and-white trail map is provided with your lift ticket.

Finding the trail: Purchase your lift ticket at Waterville Valley Base Camp, located in the town square.

Source of additional information:

Waterville Valley Base Camp
Waterville Valley, NH 03215
(800) 468-2553

Notes on the trail: Downhilling the front of the mountain was fun, but it was over too quickly. My favorite ride was down the *back*, on the Snow's Mountain Trail, to Livermore Road. This stretched the descent over a four-mile ride down a fairly easy route. It would make a pleasant uphill ride, too, which proposes the question, Why do you need a lift ticket at all?

RIDE 35 · Waterville Valley (Cross-country)

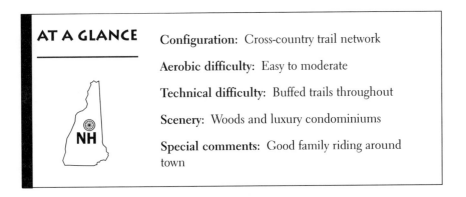

AT A GLANCE

Configuration: Cross-country trail network

Aerobic difficulty: Easy to moderate

Technical difficulty: Buffed trails throughout

Scenery: Woods and luxury condominiums

Special comments: Good family riding around town

NH

In addition to the downhilling discussed in Ride 34, Waterville Valley also has a separate system of cross-country ski trails opened for bicycles, accessed via a series of trails crisscrossing the village. The trails themselves are good, but many that appear on the ski map are closed to bikes. The ski trails in the woods have good signage (the trails in town do not). The black-and-white trail map I used is going to be replaced by a better color map (which, I'm told, will probably cost extra). As with their downhill facilities, all this comes at a price higher than what you'll pay elsewhere.

Don't get me wrong—if you're already vacationing in the Waterville Valley area and feel like riding, go ahead and do it here. You'll enjoy yourself. Those planning a New Hampshire vacation around their mountain bikes, however, should consider such cross-country trails as Gunstock, Bretton Woods, Great Glen Trails, or the Balsams first.

General location: Waterville Valley

Elevation change: Up to 400 feet of elevation gain, depending on the trails you ride

Season: Open Memorial Day weekend through Columbus Day weekend. Trail fee (in 1997): $6 ($4 for children under age 13 and seniors).

RIDE 35 · Waterville Valley (Cross-country)

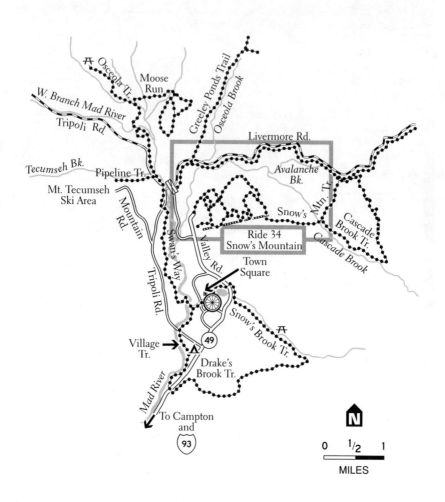

Services: Bike rentals and repairs are available on-site. All services are available in town.

Hazards: Moderate surface hazards; pedestrian traffic close to the village

Rescue index: You will be up to 2 miles from assistance.

Land status: Privately operated ski resort on U.S. Forest Service land

Maps: A black-and-white trail map is provided with your trail pass.

A brookside trail in Waterville Valley.

Finding the trail: Purchase your trail pass at Waterville Valley Base Camp, located in the town square.

Source of additional information:

Waterville Valley Base Camp
Waterville Valley, NH 03215
(800) 468-2553

RIDE 36 · Sandwich Notch

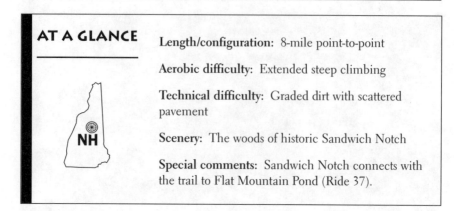

AT A GLANCE

Length/configuration: 8-mile point-to-point

Aerobic difficulty: Extended steep climbing

Technical difficulty: Graded dirt with scattered pavement

Scenery: The woods of historic Sandwich Notch

Special comments: Sandwich Notch connects with the trail to Flat Mountain Pond (Ride 37).

In the early days of the nineteenth century, Sandwich Notch was an important gateway between New Hampshire's Lakes Region and the Franconia Range of the White Mountains. When the railroads worked their way northward, however, it made more sense to take the long way around the Squam Range, a route later followed by US 3. Sandwich Notch Road lost importance and changed little over the decades. When its rustic character was threatened by development in the 1970s, a group of local citizens lobbied to have the road and its surroundings added to the White Mountain National Forest, and they were.

Sandwich Notch Road's steepest sections have been paved to minimize erosion, and some houses have sprung up on either end, but little else has changed since pioneer days. It's open to automobiles, but thanks to its rug-ged nature, sees little traffic. It's the perfect ride for getting in a little bit of history and a whole lot of climbing.

General location: Between Campton and Center Sandwich

Elevation change: There is about 1,200 feet of climbing on grades of up to 24%.

Season: Early summer through mid-fall

Services: All services can be found in West Campton (5 miles south of the northwestern trailhead on NH 49). Food can also be found in Center Sandwich, near the southeast end.

Hazards: Watch for moderate surface hazards and the occasional car. Control your speed on descents.

Rescue index: You will be up to 3 miles from inhabited areas on a lightly traveled road.

Land status: Public road on national forest land

Maps: This and other rides in the southeastern White Mountains area are included on the *White Mountain Mountain Bike Map*, which is published by the

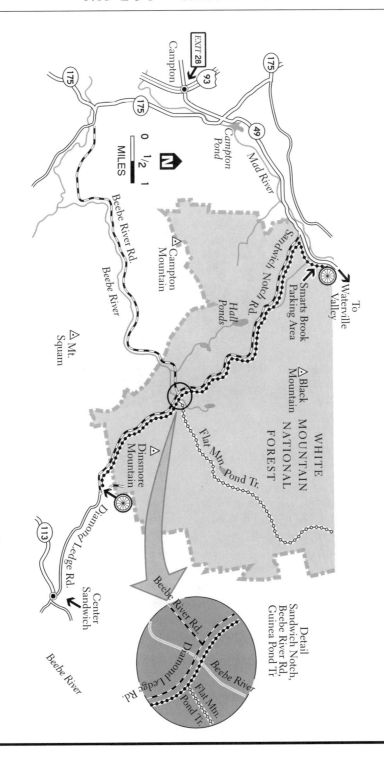

Once an important gateway to the White Mountains, Sandwich Notch has changed little since pioneer days.

Pemigewasset Ranger District of the White Mountain National Forest. It can be purchased at the Pemigewasset Ranger Station in Plymouth, or at area bike shops.

Finding the trail: The northwestern trailhead is north of West Campton. From that village, take NH 49 north 6 miles to the Smarts Brook parking area (on the right) and park. Ride about a mile back to Sandwich Notch Road, which is clearly marked.

The southeastern trailhead is 2 miles north of Center Sandwich. Take NH 113 to Center Sandwich and turn north onto Grove Street. Follow the road straight as it becomes Diamond Ledge Road and look for a wide, dirt parking area where the road to Mead Base diverges from Sandwich Notch Road (you'll see a sign pointing to Mead Base on the right).

Sources of additional information:

Pemigewasset Ranger Station
White Mountain National Forest
Route 175
Plymouth, NH 03264
(603) 536-1310

Greasey Wheel Bicycle Shop
40 South Main Street
Plymouth, NH 03264
(603) 536-3655
Mountain bikers meet here weekly for group rides.

Notes on the trail: From either trailhead, it's climb, climb, climb to the notch. By mountain bike standards, the road is pretty good, and the steepest sections have some asphalt on them to keep the erosion down. About 4.5 miles from the road's northwestern end (and about 2.5 miles from the southeastern trailhead), you'll pass Beebe River Road, which heads southwest, and the trail to Flat Mountain Pond, which goes northeast and makes an excellent mountain bike ride (see Ride 37). Sandwich Notch continues straight through both these junctions, before heading down the other side of the Sandwich Range.

RIDE 37 · Flat Mountain Pond

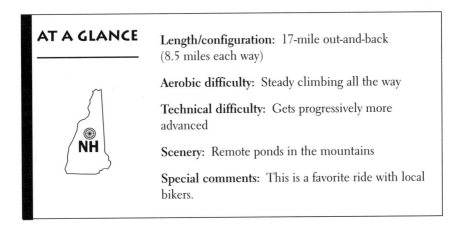

AT A GLANCE

NH

Length/configuration: 17-mile out-and-back (8.5 miles each way)

Aerobic difficulty: Steady climbing all the way

Technical difficulty: Gets progressively more advanced

Scenery: Remote ponds in the mountains

Special comments: This is a favorite ride with local bikers.

When it was established by the federal government in 1911, the White Mountain National Forest encompassed 722,000 acres. In the years since, another 41,000 acres have been appended to it, as additional pieces of forest became available (usually from timber companies looking to cash out). This area of the Sandwich Range is one of those later additions to the forest.

The ride to Flat Mountain Pond takes two trails end-to-end: the Guinea Pond Trail and the Flat Mountain Pond Trail. Hikers have traveled this route for years; it's caught on with local bikers, too. A broad trail with a gradual climb and interesting surface hazards every so often, the ride has two ponds and some lovely scenery along the way. There's even a shelter at the end to stay the night, should you wish to make an overnight trip of it.

RIDE 37 · Flat Mountain Pond

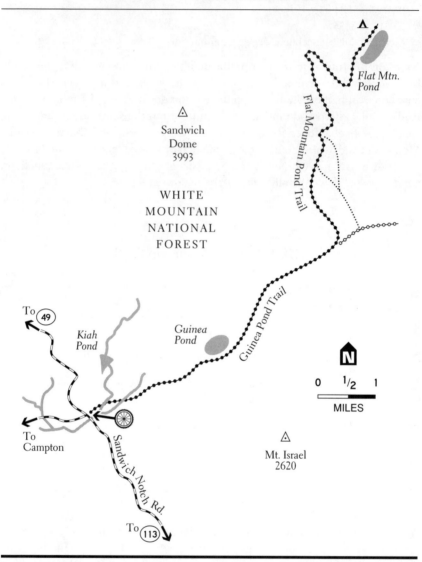

General location: 6 miles east of West Campton

Elevation change: About 1,000 feet of elevation gain, in a gradual climb that steepens toward the end; part of this trail utilizes the grade of a former logging railroad.

Season: Early summer through fall; autumn colors begin to appear in late September.

Services: There is no potable water along the route. All services can be found in West Campton, or in Plymouth, 10 miles to the south.

Hazards: Watch for pedestrians and washouts near stream crossings.

Hikers have traveled this route for years, and so can you.

Rescue index: You will be up to 10 miles from inhabited areas on a well-traveled trail.

Land status: White Mountain National Forest trails

Maps: This and other rides in the southeastern White Mountains area are included on the *White Mountain Mountain Bike Map*, which is published by the Pemigewasset Ranger District of the White Mountain National Forest. It can be purchased at the Pemigewasset Ranger Station in Plymouth, or at area bike shops.

Finding the trail: The start of the Guinea Pond Trail is located at the top of Sandwich Notch Road. A small, sandy parking area is on the road a few hundred feet southeast of the trailhead (parking here requires that you display a *Passport to the White Mountain National Forest*—see the Preface for details). As an option, park at either end of Sandwich Notch Road and ride up to the Guinea Pond trailhead for an extended ride (no *Passport* is required at either location). See Ride 36 for details on Sandwich Notch Road.

Sources of additional information:

Pemigewasset Ranger Station
White Mountain National Forest
Route 175
Plymouth, NH 03264
(603) 536-1310

Greasey Wheel Bicycle Shop
40 South Main Street
Plymouth, NH 03264
(603) 536-3655
Mountain bikers meet here weekly for group rides.

Notes on the trail: This ride is composed of two trails end-to-end: the Guinea
Pond Trail and the Flat Mountain Pond Trail. Both are signed and blazed (ignore
any side trails you see). The lower reaches of the trail are easy, as they follow an old
logging railroad bed. As you ride, the trail gets progressively tougher—you might
find yourself dismounting for mudholes, boulder fields, and washouts.

Bicycling is prohibited beyond Flat Mountain Pond—this is the edge of the
Sandwich Range Wilderness Area. The Appalachian Mountain Club maintains
a shelter at Flat Mountain Pond; primitive overnight lodging is available there
on a first-come, first-served basis.

RIDE 38 · Ridgepole Trail

AT A GLANCE

Length/configuration: 8-mile loop

Aerobic difficulty: Plenty of climbing

Technical difficulty: Challenging single-track

Scenery: Grand vistas of Squam Lake

Special comments: Convenient to both the White
Mountains and the Lakes Region

NH

The Squam Mountains are a small range tucked in between the Sandwich
Range of the White Mountains and Squam Lake. Mounts Livermore,
Webster, Morgan, Percival, Squam, and Doublehead lie along a sharp ridge that
sweeps in a broad arc from Holderness to Center Sandwich. Following this arc,
at the top of the ridge, is the Ridgepole Trail. Make no mistake—it's a challenging ride, but the payoff comes in the form of spectacular views of both the
White Mountains and Lakes Country.

This particular ride follows the Mount Webster section of the Ridgepole Trail,
as well as a variety of other trails from dirt road to single-track. All but the most experienced riders will probably have to do some walking, but don't let that discourage
you—the ride's short enough that even us less nimble types can manage it.

RIDE 38 · Ridgepole Trail

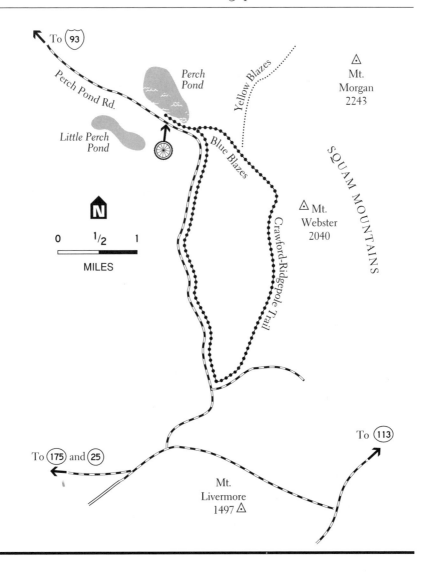

General location: Plymouth

Elevation change: About 1,400 feet of elevation gain, most of it on a steep single-track climb to Mount Webster

Season: Early summer through fall

Services: All services are available in Plymouth, 7 miles to the south.

Hazards: Watch for numerous surface hazards—rocks, roots, and windfall. Use extreme caution on descents.

It's a challenging ride, but the paybacks are great views of the White Mountains.

Rescue index: You will be up to 3 miles from inhabited areas.

Land status: Public roads and trails

Maps: *The Squam Range*, a detailed work by Bradford Washburn published by the Museum of Science, Boston, just might be the most beautiful topographic map ever made of New Hampshire geography. Ask for it at area retailers. Also see Squam Mountains quadrangle, USGS 7.5 minute series.

Finding the trail: From the Plymouth area, take NH 175 north about 5 miles and turn right just after the gift shop. Take the next right turn (about 0.3 miles) and you'll find yourself on Perch Pond Road. Go 3 miles and park in the parking area you'll see on the left, near Perch Pond.

Source of additional information:

Greasey Wheel Bicycle Shop
40 South Main Street
Plymouth, NH 03264
(603) 536-3655

Notes on the trail: From the parking area, continue on Perch Pond Road for about 2.5 miles. At the bottom of the descent, turn left onto Mountain Road and keep riding straight up until you reach the top of the ridge. There, you'll see a sign for the Crawford-Ridgepole Trail; turn left onto it, follow the yellow blazes, and keep climbing. A couple of overlooks along the way provide excellent views of Squam Lake and the surrounding countryside.

About a mile after you've crested Mount Webster, and just after a short, sharp descent, it's time to turn left onto the Cascade Trail. *Watch carefully for the junction*—it's easy to miss. (There's a small waterfall on the right.) The Cascade Trail has yellow blazes and takes you the rest of the way down the mountain. Just above Perch Pond, bear left at the fork in the trail and ride the rest of the way down to Perch Pond Road.

RIDE 39 · Reservoir Pond

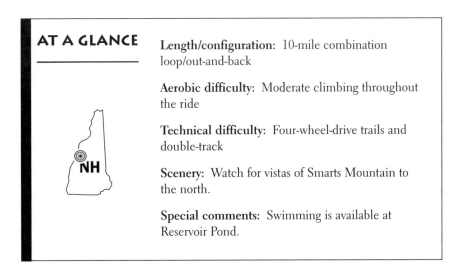

AT A GLANCE

Length/configuration: 10-mile combination loop/out-and-back

Aerobic difficulty: Moderate climbing throughout the ride

Technical difficulty: Four-wheel-drive trails and double-track

Scenery: Watch for vistas of Smarts Mountain to the north.

Special comments: Swimming is available at Reservoir Pond.

As mentioned in the Preface, the Appalachian Trail (AT) is one of the few spots in New Hampshire where mountain biking is strictly a no-no. Don't take it so hard—the AT was designed purely for foot traffic in 1921. It took nearly 16 years to complete, over the most rugged terrain between Maine and Georgia, and it has been improved ever since with tens of thousands of hours of volunteer labor. New Hampshire's portion of the trail benefits from having a particularly strong hiking club, the Appalachian Mountain Club, to supply advocacy and labor.

This ride stays off the AT (instead taking nearby dirt roads), but it does start from an AT parking area. If you're lucky, you might get the chance to hobnob with some folks on a 2,000-mile hike.

General location: Lyme

Elevation change: About 700 feet of elevation gain, with the steepest section early in the ride

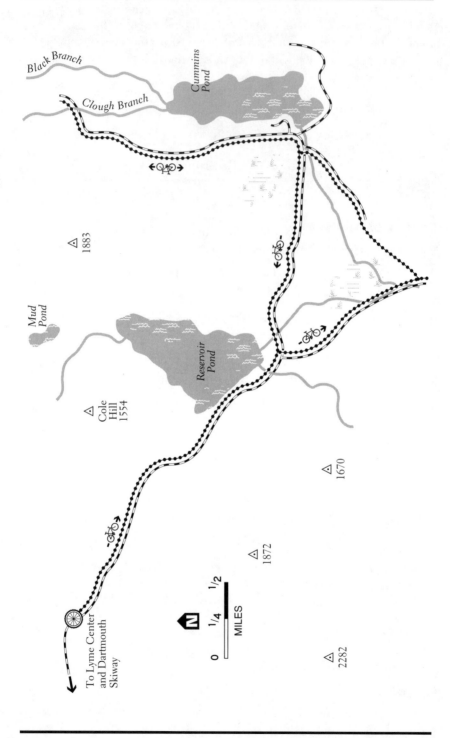

Black Branch

Clough Branch

Cummins Pond

1883

Mud Pond

Reservoir Pond

Cole Hill 1554

1670

1872

N

1/4   1/2

0   MILES

2282

To Lyme Center and Dartmouth Skiway

Season: Mid-spring through fall

Services: All services can be found in Hanover, 10 miles to the south.

Hazards: Watch for light traffic on graded dirt roads, and for surface hazards on trails.

Rescue index: You will be up to 2 miles from traveled roads or inhabited areas.

Land status: A public road, and private roads in conservation lands (mountain bikers are permitted, but please stay on the trail)

Maps: Page 38 of DeLorme's *New Hampshire Atlas and Gazetteer*. Also see Smarts Mountain quadrangle, USGS 7.5 minute series.

Finding the trail: From Lyme, turn east on the Grafton Turnpike (toward Lyme Center) and travel for about 4 miles. On the left is a parking lot where the AT goes north toward Smarts Mountain; you can park here.

Sources of additional information:

Omar & Bob's Sportshop
7 Allen Street
Hanover, NH 03755
(603) 643-3525

Tom Mowatt Cycles
213 Mechanic Street
Lebanon, NH 03766
(603) 448-5556

Notes on the trail: From the AT parking area, proceed along the road and pass Reservoir Pond on your left. Shortly past the pond, you'll see a rough, two-wheel-drive road on your right; turn right and follow it for about a mile. Just before the clearing, turn left, then left again, onto an overgrown dirt road that takes you on a northwesterly course toward Cummins Pond and the main dirt road.

When you've reached the main dirt road, turn right, then turn left onto a four-wheel-drive road along Cummins Pond. Take it as far north as you can; it becomes a hiking trail after about 1.3 miles. Turn around and head back, this time taking the main dirt road directly to Reservoir Pond and back to the AT parking area.

RIDE 40 · Loon Mountain

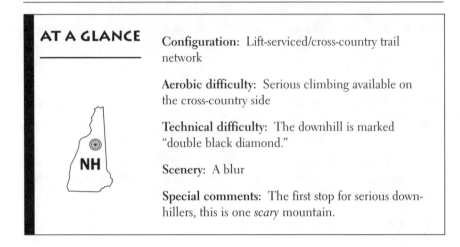

AT A GLANCE

Configuration: Lift-serviced/cross-country trail network

Aerobic difficulty: Serious climbing available on the cross-country side

Technical difficulty: The downhill is marked "double black diamond."

Scenery: A blur

Special comments: The first stop for serious down-hillers, this is one *scary* mountain.

NH

At 2,100 feet, Loon Mountain has the most vertical drop of any resort ride in this book. Double-black-diamond markers ("experts only" in ski-speak) are prominently placed at the summit to frighten off inexperienced cyclists who somehow passed the quizzing by shop employees. (I received bonus points on account of the heavy-duty drum brakes on my machine.) For those who dare, the reward is a fast, fast ride over trails that are pretty well blazed, marked, and maintained.

At Loon, you can descend directly off the mountain into the cross-country trails.

RIDE 40 · Loon Mountain

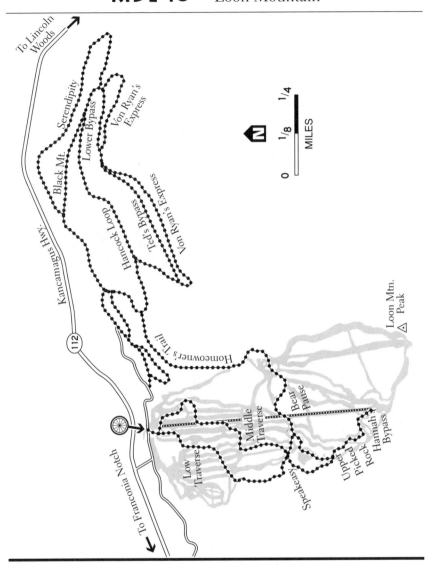

For those who opt out of the downhilling, there's a consolation prize: a modestly sized but excellent network of cross-country trails. Lower trails cut an easy path along the river; more challenging ones reach 800 feet up the side of the mountain. (Loon lets you ride them free of charge, too.) A single-color map with contours serves both systems, and a connecting trail lets you descend directly into the cross-country area.

For those who opt out of the downhilling, there are easier trails along the river.

General location: Lincoln

Elevation change: 2,100 feet of vertical drop from the summit

Season: Open daily 8:30 a.m.–5 p.m., Memorial Day weekend to Columbus Day weekend. Rates (in 1997): $12, single ride; $22, all day (discounts to those age 16 and under).

Services: Bike rentals and repairs are available on-site. All services are available in Lincoln and North Woodstock, 2 miles west.

Hazards: Keep your speed under control! There is a steep descent on the upper part of the trail, and there are waterbars and other surface hazards.

Rescue index: You are generally within a mile of assistance.

Land status: Privately operated ski resort on U.S. Forest Service land

Maps: A black-and-white trail map is provided with your lift ticket.

Finding the trail: The entrance to Loon Mountain is located about a mile east of Lincoln on the Kancamagus Highway (NH 112).

Source of additional information:

Loon Mountain Park
Lincoln, NH 03251
(603) 745-6281 ext. 5506

RIDE 41 · Lincoln Woods Trail

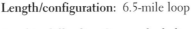
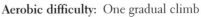

AT A GLANCE

NH

Length/configuration: 6.5-mile loop

Aerobic difficulty: One gradual climb

Technical difficulty: Easy except for one river portage (optional)

Scenery: Franconia Falls, just off the trail

Special comments: This is a very popular trail.

You've probably never heard of Elias Shay, but, in a convoluted, historical kind of way, he's the man to thank for this trail. Back in the glory days of the Industrial Revolution, Shay had a radical idea: put a "granny gear" on a steam locomotive and it would be able to climb steeper grades (sound familiar?). It worked, and his locomotive revolutionized the timber industry. Before long, Shay locomotives, and similar engines like the Heisler and the Climax, were crawling all over America's forests on hastily laid tracks, bringing freshly felled timber down to the mills. By the 1920s, though, newer machines (named after such inventors as Mr. Caterpillar and Mr. Mack) had begun to replace logging railroads, and the rails gradually disappeared. (Today, the last geared logging locomotive in the area shuffles tourists around the grounds of Clark's Trading Post in North Woodstock.)

The old East Branch & Lincoln Railroad bed follows the west bank of the Pemigewasset River. On the east bank is East Branch Road, a popular day-hiking spot for summer tourists. This ride ties them together with a portage across the river.

General location: On the Kancamagus Highway (NH 112), east of Lincoln

Elevation change: About 300 feet of elevation gain, all in one gradual climb

Season: Late spring through fall

Services: All services can be found in Lincoln, 3 miles to the west, or in North Woodstock, just beyond.

Hazards: *Watch for hikers at all times on this popular trail, especially on weekends.* Control your speed on the descent. Use caution when carrying your bike across the Pemigewasset River—if the portage looks beyond your abilities, don't attempt it; return via the trail on your side instead.

Rescue index: This trail is well traveled and patrolled by Forest Service rangers.

Land status: White Mountain National Forest trails

RIDE 41 · Lincoln Woods Trail

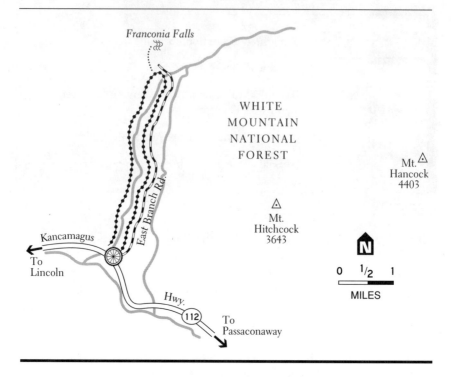

Maps: A free handout from the White Mountain National Forest provides a basic trail map and description. Also see Mount Osceola quadrangle, USGS 7.5 minute series.

Finding the trail: From Lincoln, take the Kancamagus Highway (NH 112) east about 3 miles and turn left into the Pemigewasset Wilderness parking area. Parking here requires that you display a *Passport to the White Mountain National Forest* (see the Preface for details). Or you can park in the village of Lincoln or at Loon Mountain Park (see Ride 40) and ride 2–3 miles along the Kanc to reach the trailhead.

Source of additional information:

Pemigewasset Ranger Station
White Mountain National Forest
Route 175
Plymouth, NH 03264
(603) 536-1310

Notes on the trail: From the parking area, take East Branch Road up along the river for about three miles. At the gate, turn left, carry your bike over the line of boulders across the river, cross the island and a small stream, and lift your bike up a short, steep embankment to the Lincoln Woods Trail.

In the White Mountains, even locomotives have "granny gears."

A right turn here will take you up to Franconia Falls, 0.3 mile away. Walk your bike up this portion of the trail, as it's narrow, rugged, and usually full of hikers. After you're finished sightseeing, turn around and take the Lincoln Woods Trail back down the mountain, cross the bridge over the river, and return to the parking area.

RIDE 42 · Franconia Notch State Park

AT A GLANCE

Length/configuration: 9-mile point-to-point (18 miles out-and-back)

Aerobic difficulty: Gradual climbing either way

Technical difficulty: Relax, it's paved.

Scenery: The Old Man of the Mountain and other New Hampshire landmarks

Special comments: This is a good family ride. Bring binoculars.

NH

From the Flume Visitor Center, the trail climbs gradually through the woods.

Here in Franconia Notch, the Immovable Object met the Irresistible Force. The result was a draw.

The Object? New Hampshire's beloved Old Man of the Mountain, the "great stone face" that adorns postcards, highway signs, collector plates, and airbrushed Harley-Davidson tanks throughout the state. The Old Man is just one of several natural wonders in this notch; nearby are the Flume, the Basin, Echo Lake, and other scenic delights.

The Force? America's interstate highway system, one tendril of which was set to slither right under the Old Man's nose. Not surprisingly, this upset a lot of New Hampshire folk. Construction stalled for over 15 years before the compromise you see today was agreed upon. Franconia Notch Parkway, which carries I-93 through this hallowed ground, has only 2 lanes, a 45-mph speed limit, and (more to the point for *you*) a paved, 9-mile bike path that provides easy access to Franconia's attractions.

General location: Franconia Notch, between Franconia and North Woodstock

Elevation change: Southbound, about 250 feet of altitude gain; northbound, about 750 feet. All of it is gradual.

Season: Spring through fall

Services: Water, food, and camping can be found within the park. Other services are available in North Woodstock and Franconia.

Hazards: Mixture of heavy bicycle and pedestrian traffic, especially on weekends; limited sight distances on some curves. *Please control your speed* and walk

RIDE 42 • Franconia Notch State Park

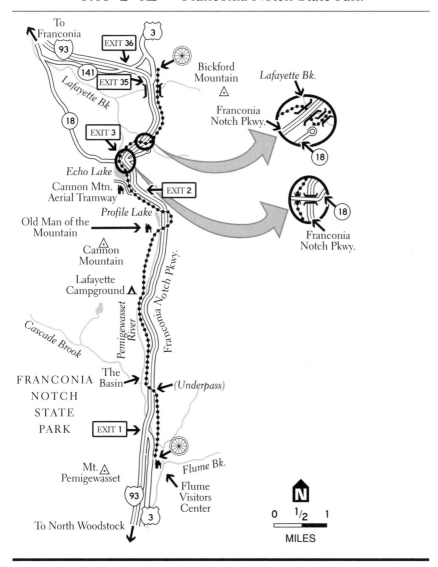

To Franconia
93
EXIT 36
3
141
EXIT 35
Lafayette Bk.
18
EXIT 3
Echo Lake
Cannon Mtn.
Aerial Tramway
EXIT 2
Profile Lake
Old Man of the
Mountain →
Cannon
Mountain
Lafayette
Campground ▲
Cascade Brook
Pemigewasset River
Franconia Notch Pkwy.
FRANCONIA
NOTCH
STATE
PARK
The
Basin →
(Underpass)
EXIT 1 →
Mt. △
Pemigewasset
93
Flume Bk.
Flume
Visitors
Center
3
To North Woodstock ↓

Bickford
Mountain △
Lafayette Bk.
Franconia
Notch Pkwy.
18
Franconia
Notch Pkwy.
18

N

0   1/2   1
MILES

your bike when so directed by signage. Use caution at underpasses and when crossing access roads.

Rescue index: You are never more than a mile from assistance, and the trail is heavily used.

Land status: State park

Maps: A trail map listing points of interest is available free at the Flume Visitor Center (southern trailhead). The Appalachian Mountain Club produces a color hiking map with contours, which can be purchased at local retailers.

With beautiful Echo Lake to your left, you'll soon ignore the parkway on your right.

Finding the trail: The southern trailhead is at the Flume Visitor Center on US 3, just north of North Woodstock. The northern trailhead is accessed via a parking area on US 3, just north of Exit 35.

Sources of additional information:

Franconia Notch State Park
Franconia, NH 03580
(603) 823-5563
Loon Mountain Park offers a shuttle service to Echo Lake
for cyclists wishing a one-way downhill ride (optional box
lunch available). Call (603) 745-6281 ext. 5506 for details.

Notes on the trail: From the Flume Visitor Center's north parking lot, the trail begins a gradual climb through wooded areas, with picnic tables placed every so often. This portion of the trail is more rustic, mostly staying in the woods. Take your time and enjoy the sights. Plan to linger at the Old Man overlook, about 5.5 miles from the start (binoculars help; the Old Man's profile is way up the side of a huge mountain).

After the Old Man, the trail levels out and begins to drop again past Echo Lake. The bridge over Lafayette Brook once carried US 3 in pre-interstate days; stop here for another excellent view. The remaining 1.5 miles of the trail utilizes the broad, straight former highway alignment to the northern trailhead on US 3. (This portion of the trail is particularly good for short rides with young children who aren't necessarily interested in seeing the landmarks farther south.)

SACO
(THE CONWAY AREA)

The Saco River is generally thought of as a Maine waterway, but its headwaters lie in New Hampshire, on the east side of Crawford Notch. The relatively small portion of the Granite State drained by the Saco is known as the Mount Washington Valley, after the 6,288-foot peak just to the northwest. This area is the eastern hub of the White Mountains. US 302, NH 16, and the Kancamagus Highway converge here, thick with tourist traffic. Any activity you'd have an urge to do on vacation is amply provided for — including, of course, mountain biking.

The Presidentials are the grandest of the White Mountain ranges, and almost too grand for mountain biking. It's impractical to take a bike up to the taller peaks (unless you register in the annual hillclimb on the Mount Washington Auto Road, held every September). The lower reaches, however, offer an abundance of off-road riding on mountain roads, ski trails, and logging paths.

Suggested Reading: *Look to the Mountain* by LeGrand Cannon, Jr. Set in pre-revolutionary days, this novel tells the story of a young pioneer couple who leave the security of the flatlands for a new life in the shadow of the White Mountains. This classic work of regional fiction recently celebrated its fiftieth year in print.

RIDE 43 · Cranmore

AT A GLANCE

Configuration: Lift-serviced trail network

Aerobic difficulty: Only your brake fingers will get a workout.

Technical difficulty: Good downhilling skills are called for.

NH

Scenery: Overlooks North Conway and the Presidential Range

Special comments: There are a dizzying array of downhill route choices.

One thing about Cranmore: the location can't be beat. It sits right at the edge of North Conway, the quintessential White Mountains tourist village. Just a short hop away you'll find a variety of restaurants, a dinner train to Crawford Notch, the Mount Washington Observatory Resource Center, and more gift and outlet shopping than you can shake a Visa card at. And don't forget the riding. I asked one man on Main Street where to find some good mountain biking. "Everywhere," he replied.

Unlike some downhill centers, which pare the route choices down to two or three, Cranmore has a large number of trails open. This isn't necessarily better: all those choices can get confusing, and I had some difficulty finding the type of long, slow trail that I like to ride. The trails feature good signage, which unfortunately is not well keyed to the trail map (I'm told that new sign-age and maps are forthcoming). Closed ski runs are cordoned, and some of the bigger waterbars have been planked over (a nice touch). Overall, Cranmore has a competent program that any experienced downhiller will want to try.

General location: North Conway

Elevation change: 1,200 feet of vertical drop from the summit

Season: Open daily 9 a.m.– 4 p.m., late June through Labor Day weekend; weekends through Columbus Day weekend. Rates (in 1997): $7, single ride; $18, all day.

Services: Bike rentals and repair are available on-site. All services are available in North Conway.

Hazards: Watch for waterbars, and keep your speed under control.

Rescue index: You are never more than a mile from assistance.

Land status: Privately owned ski resort

Maps: A two-color "bird's-eye view" map is provided with your lift ticket.

RIDE 43 · Cranmore

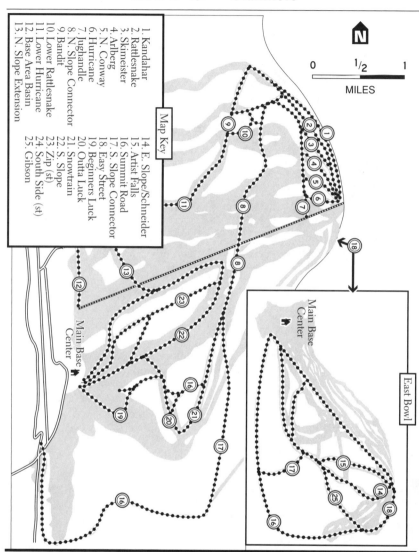

Map Key

1. Kandahar
2. Rattlesnake
3. Skimeister
4. Arlberg
5. N. Conway
6. Hurricane
7. Jughandle
8. N. Slope Connector
9. Bandit
10. Lower Rattlesnake
11. Lower Hurricane
12. Base Area Basin
13. N. Slope Extension
14. E. Slope/Schneider
15. Artist Falls
16. Summit Road
17. S. Slope Connector
18. Easy Street
19. Beginners Luck
20. Outta Luck
21. Snowtrain
22. S. Slope
23. Zip (st)
24. South Side (st)
25. Gibson

Finding the trail: From Main Street, take Kearsarge Street to Kearsarge Road, turn left, and then turn right onto Cranmore Road. Watch for the signs.

Source of additional information:

Cranmore
P.O. Box 1640
Skimobile Road
North Conway, NH 03860
(800) SUN-N-SKI

One of Cranmore's slower trails cuts across the mountain face.

RIDE 44 · Whitaker Woods

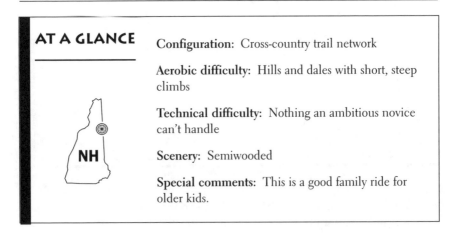

AT A GLANCE

NH

Configuration: Cross-country trail network

Aerobic difficulty: Hills and dales with short, steep climbs

Technical difficulty: Nothing an ambitious novice can't handle

Scenery: Semiwooded

Special comments: This is a good family ride for older kids.

Located just down the road from Cranmore, this undeveloped parcel of land is laced with cross-country ski trails that make for good, unstructured riding. There's no map, no signs, and no danger of getting lost. Kearsarge Road borders it on the east; a railroad track borders the west; and a power transmission line runs through the middle.

RIDE 44 · Whitaker Woods

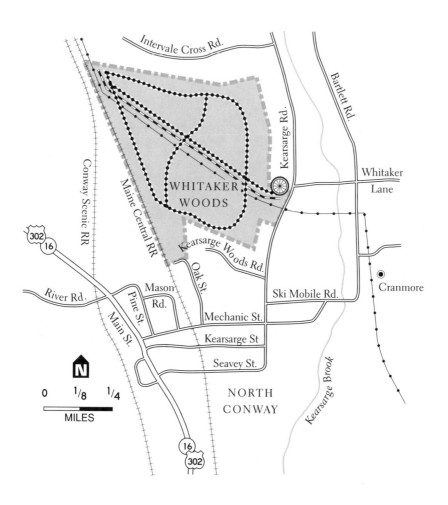

A simple out-and-back along the power line–access road yields a two-mile ride. A perimeter trail ducks into the woods, and some connecting trails link it all together. For once, you can leave the maps behind and just enjoy the trail.

General location: North Conway

Elevation change: The terrain undulates, but climbs are well under 100 feet.

Season: Late spring through fall

Navigating in Whitaker
Woods is easy; just follow
the power line.

Services: You'll find everything you need in North Conway.

Hazards: Rocks, roots, and sandy patches, none severe

Rescue index: You're within a mile of populated areas at all times.

Land status: Forest owned by the Conway Conservation Commission

Maps: None available (or necessary)

Finding the trail: There is a parking area on Kearsarge Road (just east of the village center, and north of Cranmore) at the power lines.

Source of additional information: This and other rides in the Mount Washington Valley can be found in the *Mountain Bike Guide Map*, published by Mountain Cycle Guide Service, P.O. Box 324, Intervale, NH 03845, (603) 383-9405. The latest edition is in full color and includes contours. Look for it at local bike shops.

RIDE 45 · Bartlett Experimental Forest

AT A GLANCE
───────────

NH

Configuration: Network of woods trails

Aerobic difficulty: Extended climbing

Technical difficulty: Mostly intermediate double-track

Scenery: Great views of the Presidentials; don't miss Pothole Falls.

Special comments: Orienteering skills are a *big* plus.

Frankly, I'm embarrassed. Series editor Dennis Coello is a real stickler for detailed instructions and never misses an opportunity to impress upon me that route directions should be as explicit as possible. "You gotta lead 'em by the nose," he says. (If this book hasn't gotten you lost, thank *him*, not me.) Well, on this ride, I can't do it.

Bartlett Experimental Forest is a corner of the White Mountain National Forest used in agricultural research. It's blanketed with four-wheel-drive roads and broad trails. Some appear on the USGS Bartlett topo; some don't; and none of them are marked. I met up with a group of mountain bikers at the Red Jersey Cyclery in Glen one Sunday morning, and Peter Minnich took us on a grand tour of Bartlett. (Peter is the proprietor of Mountain Cycle Guide Service and the creator of an excellent mountain biking map of the area.) We wound around various trails on the west side of Bear Mountain Road, then crossed to the east side and rode up to Pothole Falls, a beautiful series of rock formations formed by a branch of Bartlett Brook as it trickles off Table Mountain. A rapid descent through the woods took us back into town. I never looked at a map. I couldn't tell you exactly where we went. I *can* tell you that it was a great ride. (Ironically, I met Dennis for lunch afterward. "You gotta lead 'em by the nose," he told me.)

If you're good with a map and compass, obtain a copy of Peter's map or the Bartlett topo and explore the trails on your own. You won't regret it. If orienteering isn't one of your hobbies, try hooking up with a group ride, like I did, via the Red Jersey.

General location: Bartlett

Elevation change: Some trails go almost all the way up to Bear Notch, which is about 1,100 feet above the village.

Season: Early summer through fall

Services: All services can be found in Glen.

RIDE 45 · Bartlett Experimental Forest

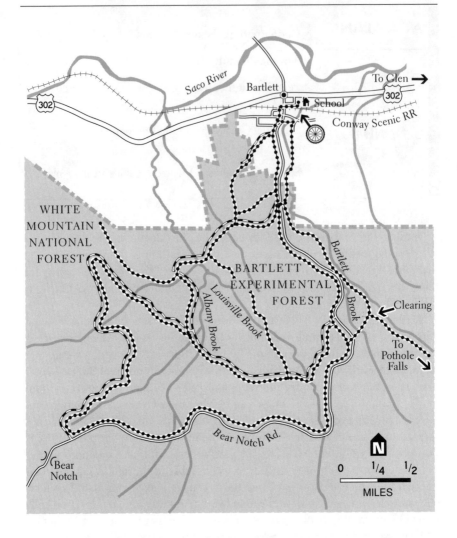

Hazards: Keep an eye out for the usual surface hazards: rocks, roots, windfall, and so on. None of it is severe.

Rescue index: You will be as far as 4 miles from town. (Bear Mountain Road is uninhabited.) Take your navigational abilities into account when planning for contingencies.

Land status: White Mountain National Forest. (Respect any posted restrictions on adjacent private land.)

Beautiful, elusive
Pothole Falls—well
worth the search.

Maps: Bartlett quadrangle, USGS 7.5 minute series. Also see the *Mountain Bike Guide Map*, published by Mountain Cycle Guide Service, P.O. Box 324, Intervale, NH 03845, (603) 383-9405. The latest edition is in full color and includes contours. Ask for it at the Red Jersey.

Finding the trail: Park at the school in Bartlett, one block south of US 302. Ride up Bear Mountain Road and watch for any one of several unmarked roads on either side.

Source of additional information:

> Red Jersey Cyclery
> P.O. Box 1209
> Route 302
> Glen, NH 03838
> (603) 383-4660
> Mountain bikers meet here for weekly rides on Sunday mornings.

Notes on the trail: Like I said, I can't give detailed directions. Here's what I know: Bear Mountain Road is the only pavement you'll see south of US 302;

If navigation isn't one of your skills, try hooking up with a group ride.

keep it in mind as a navigational aid and potential bailout route. Pothole Falls is somewhere uphill from the big clearing on the east side of Bear Mountain Road. In the course of a morning ride with the group, I racked up 9.1 miles and 550 feet of elevation gain. Hansel-n-Gretel brand florescent-orange bread crumbs are available in convenient trail-size bags at the Red Jersey. Have fun!

RIDE 46 · Sawyer River

AT A GLANCE

NH

Length/configuration: 14-mile out-and-back (7 miles each way)

Aerobic difficulty: Gradual climbing throughout the ride

Technical difficulty: Varies from easy to moderately challenging

Scenery: Wooded valley deep in the national forest

Special comments: This route might be turned into an aggressive 26-mile loop (see below).

RIDE 46 · Sawyer River

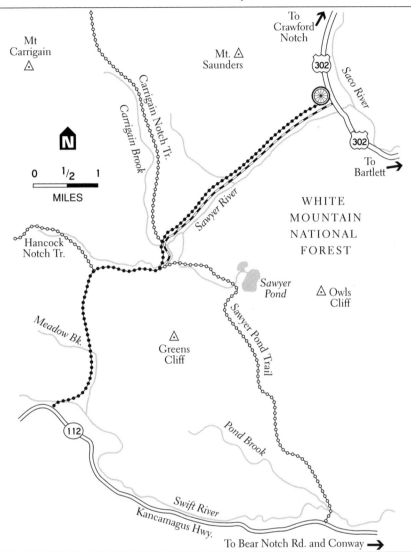

Mt
Carrigain

Mt.
Saunders

To
Crawford
Notch

302

Saco River

302

To
Bartlett

WHITE
MOUNTAIN
NATIONAL
FOREST

Carrigain Notch Tr.

Carrigain Brook

Sawyer River

Hancock
Notch Tr.

Sawyer
Pond

Owls
Cliff

Sawyer Pond Trail

Meadow Bk.

Greens
Cliff

112

Pond Brook

Swift River
Kancamagus Hwy.

To Bear Notch Rd. and Conway →

0   1/2   1
MILES

Deep in the heart of the White Mountains, this ride follows the Sawyer River along a gap between the peaks from US 302 to the Kancamagus Highway. The first half of the ride utilizes an open dirt road; the trail beyond is more rustic and mostly follows an old logging railroad grade. Other trails crisscross the area, and many of them make good riding, but you'll want to obtain a good trail map first (ask at area retailers).

General location: Bartlett

Deep in the White Mountains, the Sawyer River cuts through the woods to reach the Saco.

Elevation change: About 1,000 feet of elevation gain

Season: Early summer through fall

Services: Services can be found in Bartlett, Glen, or Conway, to the east on US 302.

Hazards: Surface hazards abound throughout the trail.

Rescue index: Assistance will be up to 4 miles away; make sure you are adequately prepared for wilderness.

Land status: White Mountain National Forest trails

Maps: The *Mountain Bike Guide Map,* published by Mountain Cycle Guide Service, P.O. Box 324, Intervale, NH 03845, (603) 383-9405. The latest edition is in full color and includes contours. Also see Bartlett and Mount Carrigan quadrangles, USGS 7.5 minute series.

Finding the trail: From Conway, take US 302 west. About 3.5 miles beyond Bartlett, you'll see Sawyer River Road on your left; park in the wide dirt area at the corner. (Parking here requires that you display a *Passport to the White Mountain National Forest*—see the Preface for details. Or you can park in Glen or Bartlett and ride US 302 to the trailhead.)

Sources of additional information:

Red Jersey Cyclery
P.O. Box 1209
Route 302
Glen, NH 03838
(603) 383-4660
Mountain bikers meet here for weekly rides on Sunday mornings.

Saco Ranger Station
White Mountain National Forest
Kancamagus Highway
Conway, NH 03818
(603) 447-5448

Appalachian Mountain Club
Pinkham Notch Camp
P.O. Box 298
Pinkham Notch, NH 03581
(603) 466-2725

Notes on the trail: From the parking area, follow Sawyer River Road for about four miles to the gate and proceed past it. About a mile beyond the gate, watch for the junction with the Sawyer River Trail and turn left onto it. Follow it southward along the brook. About a half mile before the end of the trail, it begins climbing again. You end up on the Kancamagus Highway, about 17 miles west of Conway. Turn around and retrace your trail.

You can loop back to your starting point on paved roads as an alternative ride. Turn left onto the Kanc, ride it for about seven miles to Bear Notch Road, and turn left. Over its eight-mile length, Bear Notch Road climbs nearly 600 feet before descending into Bartlett. From there, turn left onto US 302 to return to your starting point.

RIDE 47 · Doublehead

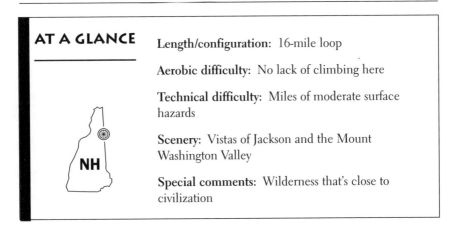

AT A GLANCE

Length/configuration: 16-mile loop

Aerobic difficulty: No lack of climbing here

Technical difficulty: Miles of moderate surface hazards

Scenery: Vistas of Jackson and the Mount Washington Valley

Special comments: Wilderness that's close to civilization

NH

The US 302 corridor between Glen and Conway is an awfully busy place, for the country. Lining the highway is a dizzying selection of theme parks, fine restaurants, outlet stores, and motor inns in every category from "excellent" to "way too excellent." You and everybody else came up here to get away from "it all," yet here "it all" is.

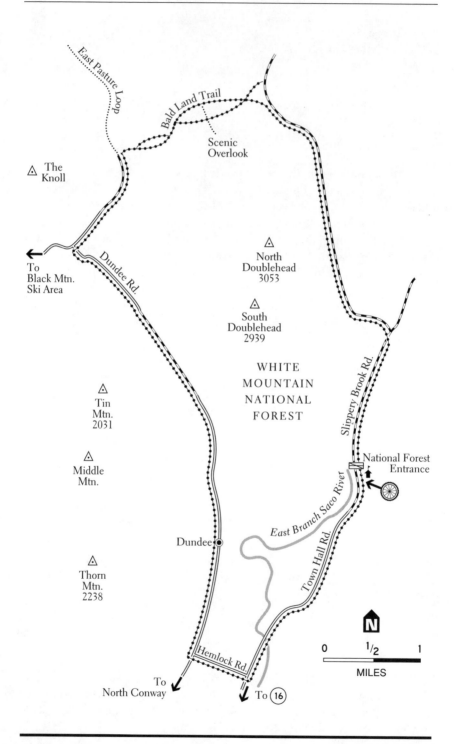

East Pasture Loop

Bald Land Trail

Scenic
Overlook

△ The
Knoll

← To
Black Mtn.
Ski Area

Dundee Rd.

△
North
Doublehead
3053

△
South
Doublehead
2939

WHITE
MOUNTAIN
NATIONAL
FOREST

Slippery Brook Rd.

National Forest
Entrance

△
Tin
Mtn.
2031

△
Middle
Mtn.

East Branch Saco River

Town Hall Rd.

Dundee ⊙

△
Thorn
Mtn.
2238

N

0   1/2   1

MILES

Hemlock Rd.

To
North Conway

To (16)

Signs of civilization fall behind quickly in the White Mountain National Forest.

Don't despair. Follow the East Branch of the Saco into the forest, and signs of civilization fall behind pretty quickly. This loop around the twin peaks of Doublehead starts on the outskirts of Jackson and heads into the wilderness on a combination of pavement, graded dirt, double-track, and single-track trails, climbing for much of the way, with the undeveloped wooded slopes of the White Mountain National Forest as your backdrop. This ride is one good way to get the blare of the Mount Washington Valley out of your ears for a few hours, before rejoining civilization again.

General location: Jackson

Elevation change: About 1,400 feet of climbing, mostly over a steady 6-mile ascent

Season: Early summer through fall

Services: Restaurants and lodging can be found in Jackson. All services can be found in North Conway.

Hazards: Watch for waterbars and other surface hazards on trails, and control your speed during descents. Keep an eye out for the occasional car on the dirt roads.

Rescue index: You will be up to 8 miles from assistance. Make sure you are adequately prepared for wilderness.

Land status: White Mountain National Forest roads and trails; public roads

Maps: The *Mountain Bike Guide Map,* published by Mountain Cycle Guide Service, P.O. Box 324, Intervale, NH 03845, (603) 383-9405. The latest edition is in full color and includes contours. Also see Jackson and Chatham quadrangles, USGS 7.5 minute series.

Finding the trail: From Glen take NH 16 south 1.5 miles to Town Hall Road and turn left. Follow the road along the East Branch of the Saco River for 3 miles, and bear left onto Slippery Brook Road, which is unpaved. At the gate that marks the edge of White Mountain National Forest land, pull into one of the parking areas on either side.

Sources of additional information:

Saco Ranger Station
White Mountain National Forest
Kancamagus Highway
Conway, NH 03818
(603) 447-5448

Joe Jones Ski and Sports
Main Street
North Conway, NH 03860
(603) 356-9411

Notes on the trail: From the gate, continue up the road for two miles before turning left. Proceed another 2.5 miles, cross a small bridge over East Branch, and bear left onto a grassy trail. A half-mile ride with some short but steep climbs will take you to the Bald Land Trail; turn left onto it and continue climbing. At the saddle, the highest point on this ride, turn left to follow the trail marked "East Pasture Loop to Jackson." The trail descends sharply from here; keep left at all trail junctions until you reach Dundee Road at a **T** intersection. Turn left and follow Dundee Road for about four miles. Watch for a condominium complex, and immediately after it turn left onto Hemlock Road. Bear right at Vista Lane to reach Town Hall Road, and turn left to return to the starting point.

ANDROSCOGGIN
(THE GORHAM AREA)

Gorham sits on the border between the White Mountains' vacationland and the workaday world of the North Country. It's the last New Hampshire town on the Appalachian Trail and home to the northernmost ranger station of the White Mountain National Forest. The Carter/Moriah Range of the White Mountains is just south of town, and east of Pinkham Notch. Not far from Gorham to the west, over a broad gap in the mountains, lies the Ammonoosuc valley, which drains the northern halves of Franconia and Crawford Notches.

As you ride in the Androscoggin valley, make no comments about the odor. What you smell is the paper mill. Residents aren't particularly fond of the scent, either, but paper-making is a *big* industry here, and that smell means jobs and money. New Hampshire has been a paper-producing state for over 200 years. When captured German soldiers arrived at a converted Civilian Conservation Corps (CCC) camp in nearby Stark during World War II, they were put to work cutting cordwood for the mills. Many of the trails used by mountain bikers here were first cut as logging roads. They traverse a mix of federal land and corporate-owned properties, and thus far, trail conflicts haven't been a problem.

Suggested Reading: *Stark Decency: German Prisoners of War in a New England Village* by Allen V. Koop. Books on the role of Germany in World War II have a habit of wedging their way onto my bookshelves. This one details the history of the aforementioned POW camp, including the unlikely friendships that developed between prisoners and townsfolk.

RIDE 48 · Bretton Woods (Lift-serviced)

AT A GLANCE

Configuration: Lift-serviced trail network

Aerobic difficulty: Even Issac Newton could do it.

Technical difficulty: Requires utilization of your downhilling skills

Scenery: From the summit, an unbroken view of the Presidential Range

NH

Special comments: Bring your binoculars.

Bretton Woods is a fine place for downhilling, but it's the *surroundings* I just can't get off my mind. Stand at the top of the chairlift and you'll see why. Here, you have a panoramic view of the entire Presidential Range. Whip out your binoculars and take a look; those puffs of steam up the big mountain belong to the hard-working little engines of the Mount Washington Cog Railway. Down below is the Mount Washington Hotel, one of the few surviving grand resort hotels of that bygone age before Howard Johnson. Spectacular Crawford Notch lies just a few miles to the east.

Ahh . . . but back to the trails. It's hard to find fault with Bretton's program: nicely laid-out trail system, good signage, reasonable lift ticket. Their full-color map (with its obtuse number-coding for trails) is adequate, with an even better one on the way. The long, slow trail that I favored was a little rougher than I prefer, but to be fair to Bretton, this one does cross over into national forest land, and there are restrictions there on what can be done with the trail.

General location: Bretton Woods

Elevation change: 1,300 feet of vertical drop

Season: Open 10 a.m.–4:30 p.m. weekends, Memorial Day weekend through late June; daily through Columbus Day weekend. Rates (in 1997): $5, single ride; $15, all day.

Services: Bike rentals and repairs are available on-site. Other services are avail able in Bretton Woods and in Twin Mountain, 4 miles west on US 302.

Hazards: Watch for waterbars and other surface hazards; keep your speed under control.

Rescue index: You are generally within a mile of assistance.

Land status: Privately owned ski resort

Maps: A full-color "bird's-eye view" map is provided with your lift ticket.

RIDE 48 · Bretton Woods (Lift-serviced)

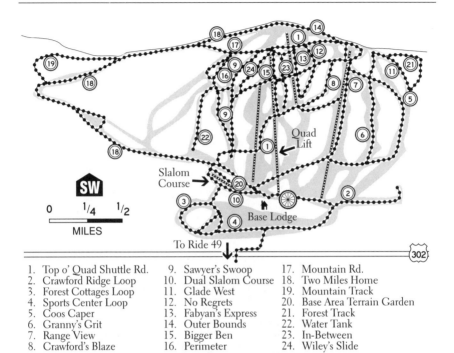

1. Top o' Quad Shuttle Rd.
2. Crawford Ridge Loop
3. Forest Cottages Loop
4. Sports Center Loop
5. Coos Caper
6. Granny's Grit
7. Range View
8. Crawford's Blaze
9. Sawyer's Swoop
10. Dual Slalom Course
11. Glade West
12. No Regrets
13. Fabyan's Express
14. Outer Bounds
15. Bigger Ben
16. Perimeter
17. Mountain Rd.
18. Two Miles Home
19. Mountain Track
20. Base Area Terrain Garden
21. Forest Track
22. Water Tank
23. In-Between
24. Wiley's Slide

Finding the trail: Bretton Woods is on US 302, opposite the Cog Railway base road.

Source of additional information:

Ski Bretton Woods
Route 302
Bretton Woods, NH 03575
(800) 232-2972

The "Two Miles Home" trail is the easiest, and longest, way to descend Bretton Woods' mountain.

RIDE 49 · Bretton Woods (Cross-country)

AT A GLANCE
——————

NH

Configuration: Cross-country trail network

Aerobic difficulty: Good climbs aren't hard to find.

Technical difficulty: Keep on your toes.

Scenery: Woods, golf course

Special comments: Don't miss the "tunnel" trail.

Just across the road from the downhilling mentioned in Ride 48, Bretton Woods also has a cross-country trail system. Not all the trails are open to bikes, but most are, and they include some pretty good ones. One of the prettiest is the

RIDE 49 · Bretton Woods (Cross-country)

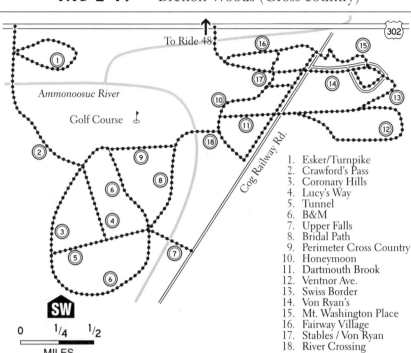

1. Esker/Turnpike
2. Crawford's Pass
3. Coronary Hills
4. Lucy's Way
5. Tunnel
6. B&M
7. Upper Falls
8. Bridal Path
9. Perimeter Cross Country
10. Honeymoon
11. Dartmouth Brook
12. Ventnor Ave.
13. Swiss Border
14. Von Ryan's
15. Mt. Washington Place
16. Fairway Village
17. Stables / Von Ryan
18. River Crossing

Tunnel Trail, a winding path through dense pines. (It's about the same length as a real tunnel in Pennsylvania I biked through, but *far* more enjoyable.)

At the outer fringes, the trail is rustic, with some erosion around waterbars. Closer in, things are smoother—too smooth, in fact, around the golf course, where the trail on the map seems to vanish into the green. Good signage can be found at the junctions, with blue-diamond blazes in between to keep you on track.

General location: Bretton Woods

Elevation change: Up to 400 feet of elevation gain from the lowest point

Season: Open 10 a.m.–4:30 p.m. weekends, Memorial Day weekend through late June; daily through Columbus Day weekend. Rates (in 1997): $4.

Services: Bike rentals and repairs are available on-site. Other services are available in Bretton Woods and in Twin Mountain, 4 miles west on US 302.

Hazards: On the outer trails, watch for waterbars and washouts. Watch for flying white balls in the vicinity of the golf course.

Rescue index: You are generally within a mile of assistance.

Land status: Privately owned ski resort

Good trail signage and
blazing keep you on
track in Bretton Woods.

Maps: A full-color map is provided with your lift ticket. (Ask for a copy of the cross-country ski map as well; it's more detailed and includes contour lines.)

Finding the trail: Bretton Woods is on US 302, opposite the Cog Railway base road. Follow the "Ski Bretton Woods" sign to the base lodge, and stop in for a permit and a trail map.

Source of additional information:

Ski Bretton Woods
Route 302
Bretton Woods, NH 03575
(800) 232-2972

RIDE 50 · Cherry Mountain

AT A GLANCE

NH

Length/configuration: 27-mile loop

Aerobic difficulty: Serious climbing in the shadow of Mount Washington

Technical difficulty: Good dirt roads throughout

Scenery: The spectacular Presidential Range

Special comments: This is a hillclimber's delight.

Right in the middle of the Presidentials, Jefferson Notch is one of the lesser-known notches in the White Mountains, not through any fault of its own, but because it lies perpendicular to prevailing traffic patterns. Cresting at 3,007 feet, Jefferson Notch Road is the highest public road in New Hampshire (the Mount Washington Auto Road, which rises to 6,288 feet, is a privately owned toll road). Its dirt surface is maintained enough to be drivable—at least in summertime—and the scenery is spectacular. When you ask a Forest Service ranger where to ride, this is the first spot they'll point you to.

The famous Mount Washington Cog Railway—no mountain is too high when you've got the right gearing.

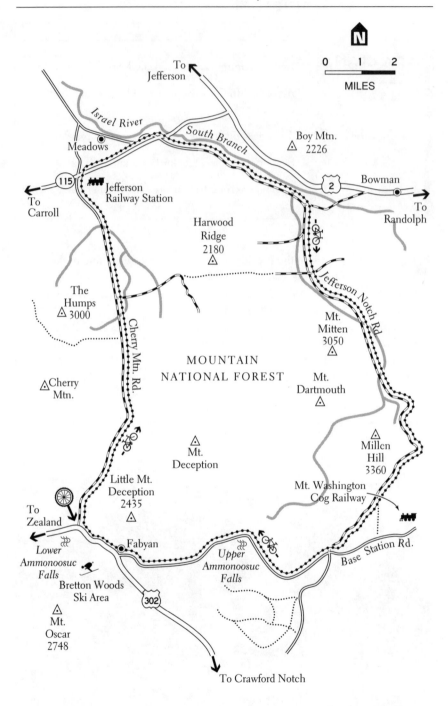

The Forest Service's handout describes a slightly different ride than what I've mapped here; the northern leg cuts through the forest on Mount Mitten Road. There's nothing wrong with that route, but this one continues down into the Israel River valley and picks up a dirt road that's somewhat smoother, for a ride that's less technical and more vertical. Pick whichever version suits your mood.

General location: Fabyan, on US 302

Elevation change: About 2,500 feet of elevation gain throughout the ride

Season: Early summer through fall. (Jefferson Notch Road is closed during the winter and spring.)

Services: Food, camping, and lodging are available along US 302 between Twin Mountain and Bretton Woods. Bike repairs and accessories are available at Ski Bretton Woods (see Rides 48 and 49).

Hazards: Watch for traffic on all roads, especially when descending.

Rescue index: You will be as far as 5 miles from inhabited areas.

Land status: Public roads

Maps: A free handout from the White Mountain National Forest provides a basic trail map and description; look for it at any ranger station. Also look for any one of the Mount Washington–area topographic maps published by various organizations and sold widely in area stores.

Finding the trail: From Twin Mountain, take US 302 east 3 miles to a parking area on the left, about 600 feet east of the Zealand Campground. Parking here requires that you display a *Passport to the White Mountain National Forest*—see the Preface for details. If you're staying in nearby lodging, you may wish to ride your bike to the trailhead.

Sources of additional information:

Ammonoosuc Ranger Station
White Mountain National Forest
Box 239
Trudeau Road
Bethlehem, NH 03574
(603) 869-2626

Ski Bretton Woods
Route 302
Bretton Woods, NH 03575
(800) 232-2972

Notes on the trail: From the parking area, take US 302 a short distance to Cherry Mountain Road and follow it north for seven miles. When you reach NH 115, turn right and follow it for about two miles. Immediately after the old railroad grade, turn right onto Valley Road, which is gravel, and follow it along the south branch of the Israel River for about three miles. Turn right onto Jefferson Notch Road and start climbing—you'll be gaining 1,600 feet of elevation over the next

5.5 miles. Over the notch lies a steep 3.5-mile descent to the junction with Base Station Road, where you'll turn right. (A left turn takes you to the base station of the famous Mount Washington Cog Railway, living proof that no mountain is too high when you've got the right gearing.) Descend gently on Base Station Road to US 302; turn right and ride the rest of the way to your starting point.

RIDE 51 · Wild River

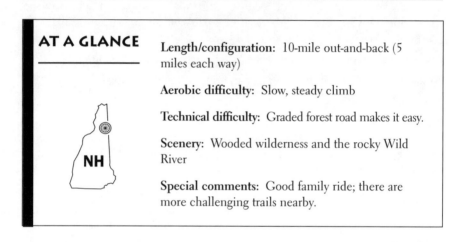

AT A GLANCE

Length/configuration: 10-mile out-and-back (5 miles each way)

Aerobic difficulty: Slow, steady climb

Technical difficulty: Graded forest road makes it easy.

Scenery: Wooded wilderness and the rocky Wild River

Special comments: Good family ride; there are more challenging trails nearby.

I'm bending the rules a bit for this easy ride; the trailhead is actually in the state of Maine. A graded forest road takes you back across the state line and along the east shore of the Wild River. Once upon a time, this was a logging railroad; now this quiet corner of the White Mountains serves up a primitive White Mountain National Forest campsite, a favorite fishing spot, and several hiking trails.

Look closely as you ride, and you'll see places where, for a more direct route, the road has deviated from the old railroad bed. When you reach the campground, hike over to the Wild River and admire its many huge boulders (souvenirs left by a departing glacier after the last ice age). To the northwest you'll see the peaks of the Carter/Moriah Range, a ridge that is traversed by the Appalachian Trail on its way to Gorham and its eventual terminus in Maine.

General location: Gilead, Maine (10 miles east of Gorham on US 2)

Elevation change: The trail gains about 300 feet in a very gradual ascent.

Season: Early summer through fall

Services: Primitive camping is available at a White Mountain National Forest site along the route. Other services can be found in Gorham, 10 miles east on US 2.

Hazards: Watch for light vehicular traffic on the road.

RIDE 51 · Wild River

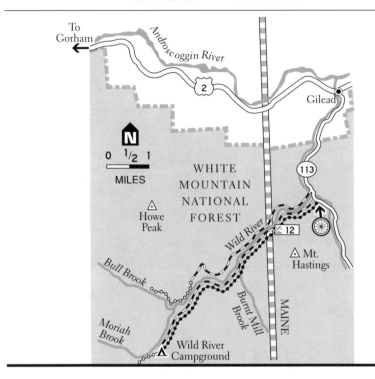

Rescue index: Assistance will be several miles away, but you will be on a road that sees regular use.

Land status: White Mountain National Forest road

Maps: Page 49 of DeLorme's *New Hampshire Atlas and Gazetteer*. Also see Wild River quadrangle, USGS 7.5 minute series.

Finding the trail: From Gorham, take US 2 east to ME 113 (the first right turn after the state line). Drive south for about 2.5 miles. A White Mountain National Forest parking area is on the right, adjacent to the dirt road. (A *Passport to the White Mountain National Forest* is required; see Preface for details.)

Source of additional information: White Mountain National Forest, Androscoggin Ranger Station (on NH 16 about 2 miles south of Gorham)

Notes on the trail: The trail is about as easy to follow as it gets: it's the only graded dirt road around. After you're rested up, turn around and enjoy a gentle downhill ride back to the parking area. The Wild River's west shore has hiking trails to the peaks beyond, but unfortunately, the only bridge south of US 2 across the river is, at this writing, out (you pass its piers about two miles into the ride), and the boulders make fording (especially with a bike) a tricky and possibly dangerous operation.

Somewhere east of the border along the Wild River.

RIDE 52 · The Pipeline

AT A GLANCE
_____

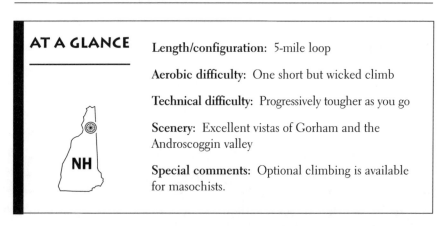

NH

Length/configuration: 5-mile loop

Aerobic difficulty: One short but wicked climb

Technical difficulty: Progressively tougher as you go

Scenery: Excellent vistas of Gorham and the Androscoggin valley

Special comments: Optional climbing is available for masochists.

The exact year has been lost to the mists of time, but legend has it that Ignatz Schwinn was still alive when a forward-thinking group of New England cyclists decided to build an off-road bicycling trail through the quiet town of Gorham. Incorporating themselves as the Portland Pipeline Company, they quickly secured a right-of-way, purchased some secondhand earth-moving equipment, and set to work building the finest mountain biking trail the world

RIDE 52 · The Pipeline

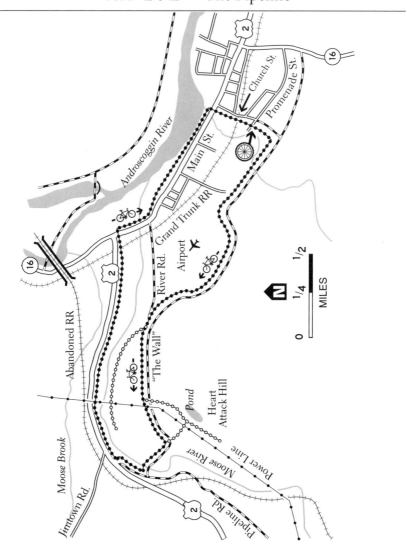

had ever seen. Skeptics called them crazy at first, but with the invention of the knobby tire some years later . . .

Okay, so I'm lying. The truth is, the Portland Pipeline people are in the crude oil business, but they won't object to you using their access road for mountain biking. The road is mostly level, but watch out for a hill at the western end so aptly named "the Wall." Gluttons for punishment are welcome to treat them-

The pipeline's right-of-way cuts a broad swath through the trees.

selves to the optional "Heart Attack Hill" before crossing the river and returning to the starting point via village streets.

General location: Gorham

Elevation change: The ride includes a 100-foot climb you won't forget (and more if you want).

Season: Early summer through fall

Services: All services can be found in Gorham.

Hazards: Watch for moderate surface hazards, a couple of muddy spots, and occasional ATVs. Use caution when descending. Use care in traffic when riding on village streets.

Rescue index: You're never more than a mile from the village.

Land status: Privately owned pipeline right-of-way

Maps: *Mountain Biking in the Northern White Mountains*, published by Venture Project, P.O. Box 892, Bethel, ME 04217, (207) 824-3083. This map of rides in the Gorham area was compiled by Mike Micucci, proprietor of Moriah Sports.

Finding the trail: From Main Street in Gorham, turn south onto Church Street (it does not extend north), take it to the end, and park on Promenade Street. Access to the pipeline is next to the U.S. Forest Service maintenance depot.

Source of additional information:

Moriah Sports
101 Main Street
Gorham, NH 03581
(603) 466-5050
Proprietor Mike Micucci is the area's authority on mountain biking.

Notes on the trail: From your parking spot on Promenade Street, follow the access road past the Forest Service garage for a short distance to the pipeline right-of-way. Turn right onto the four-wheel-drive road and follow the pipeline (it's underground, but its right-of-way cuts a broad, straight swath through the trees). Follow the road as it swings to the left and crosses over a small rise. To your left, you'll see a small area used as an obstacle course by local ATVers; continue west along the dirt road, through a patch of trees, and across the pipeline again to the other side. On the left you'll see a large signboard, with a message on the other side greeting visiting snowmobilers. Bear left to stay with the pipeline; you should see the Wall just ahead. Go for it!

Enjoying the climb? Then look for a trail on your left underneath the power line—this is the optional Heart Attack Hill. Otherwise, crest the Wall and take in a marvelous view of the Moose River valley. Ride ahead and turn right for the descent, "Headplant Hill" (who came up with these names, anyway?). As the name suggests, use caution. At the bottom, cross the wooden bridge, ride up the embankment to US 2, and take a right. At the traffic light at Main Street, turn right, ride to Church Street, and return to where you parked.

RIDE 53 · Cascade Falls

<table>
<tr>
<td>AT A GLANCE</td>
<td>Length/configuration: 9.6-mile out-and-back (4.8 miles each way)</td>
</tr>
<tr>
<td rowspan="2">NH</td>
<td>Aerobic difficulty: A mostly level ride</td>
</tr>
<tr>
<td>Technical difficulty: Progressively more technical</td>
</tr>
<tr>
<td></td>
<td>Scenery: Views along the Androscoggin River</td>
</tr>
<tr>
<td></td>
<td>Special comments: This ride may be linked with Ride 54.</td>
</tr>
</table>

It doesn't take you on an old logging road, but *next* to one, in a manner of speaking. "All up the lakes . . ." wrote Louise Rich in 1942, "the winter's cut of four-foot pulpwood lies boomed on the thick ice, waiting for the spring break-up. Before the first step of the metamorphosis from so many sticks of wood to so many Sunday Supplements, or high explosives, or evening gowns can begin, it must be got to the mills in Berlin, N.H., on the Androscoggin. The obvious method is to float the wood down." And so they did, but not anymore. Trucks handle the work.

Even though the Androscoggin has lost its usefulness as a means of timber transport, it's lost none of its charm (and the water quality has improved markedly, too). This flat ride along the east bank, just downstream of the mill, has some challenging spots and enough scenery to make it worth your while.

General location: Gorham

Elevation change: The ride is flat for most of the way, with some short technical climbs at the north end.

Season: Early summer through fall

Services: All services can be found in Gorham.

Hazards: Watch for surface hazards on the northern portion of this ride.

Rescue index: You will be within 1 mile of inhabited areas throughout the ride.

Land status: Town roads; railroad bed

Maps: *Mountain Biking in the Northern White Mountains*, published by Venture Project, P.O. Box 892, Bethel, ME 04217, (207) 824-3083. This map of rides in the Gorham area was compiled by Mike Micucci, proprietor of Moriah Sports. Also see Berlin quadrangle, USGS 7.5 minute series.

Finding the trail: From Gorham, take NH 16 north. On the edge of town, the road passes underneath a tall steel railroad trestle. Park in the broad parking area under the trestle, on your right.

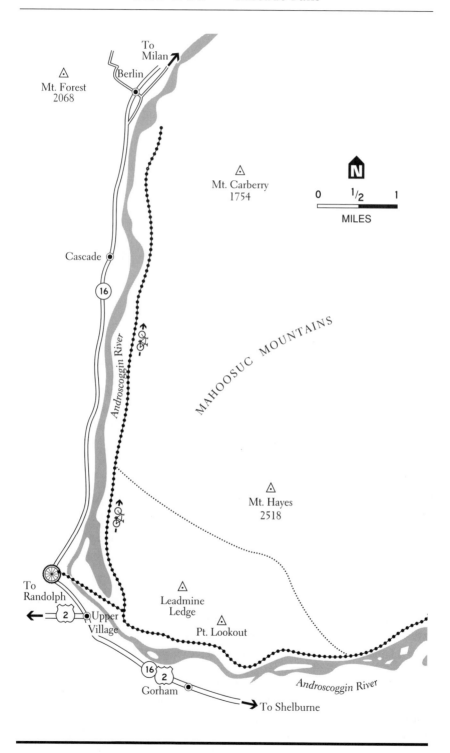

Source of additional information:

Moriah Sports
101 Main Street
Gorham, NH 03581
(603) 466-5050
Proprietor Mike Micucci is the area's authority on mountain biking.

Notes on the trail: From the parking area, walk your bike across the railroad trestle's pedestrian walkway (watch your head). On the far side, turn right and ride the dirt road to the paper company's dam on the Androscoggin River. Cross the dam by riding between the brick powerhouse and the wooden sheds to the left. Once on the east shore, turn left and follow the dirt road north along the riverbank.

As you approach the falls, the trail gets progressively narrower and rougher. Be prepared to walk if necessary at a couple of short, sharp hills. When you've had enough, turn around and check out the Leadmine Ledge Trail (see next ride).

RIDE 54 · Leadmine Ledge

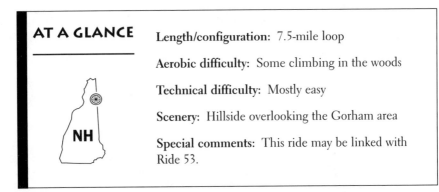

AT A GLANCE

Length/configuration: 7.5-mile loop

Aerobic difficulty: Some climbing in the woods

Technical difficulty: Mostly easy

Scenery: Hillside overlooking the Gorham area

Special comments: This ride may be linked with Ride 53.

Both Ride 53 and 54 take you across the Androscoggin River on a dam operated by Crown Vantage, which owns the paper mill upstream in Berlin. A brick powerhouse of early twentieth-century vintage also straddles the river there, converting the force of gravity acting on the water into electric current. Stop on the dam and you can peer through the powerhouse's upper windows down to the generating floor.

Fascinating places, powerhouses. Admittedly, no moving parts are visible (the turbines themselves are under the floor). A row of huge generators sit there on a pristine gray-painted floor, doing their work at a seeming standstill. You can hear them whine, hear the rush of water as it exits the races, hear the hum of the

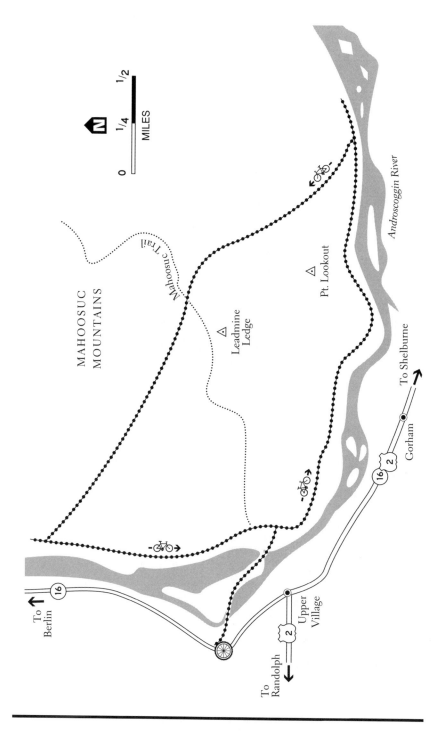

MAHOOSUC
MOUNTAINS

Mahoosuc Trail

Androscoggin River

Leadmine
Ledge

Pt. Lookout

N

0   1/4   1/2
MILES

To
Berlin

16

To
Randolph

Upper
Village

2

16 2

Gorham

To Shelburne

A logging road takes you
up the hill overlooking
Gorham.

transformers outside as they step up the voltage for transmission over high-tension lines. Hydroelectric power accounts for about one-fifth of New Hampshire's power generation. One look at a little powerhouse like this, clean, quiet, and paid for, makes me wonder why they ever built that infamous nuclear plant down in Seabrook.

General location: Gorham

Elevation change: The ride has one steady climb of 900 feet, a matching descent, and a lot of level riding.

Season: Early summer through fall

Services: All services can be found in Gorham.

Hazards: Watch for surface hazards on the single-track portion of the ride, and use caution on the descent.

Rescue index: You will be up to 2 miles from inhabited areas.

Land status: Private and public roads

Maps: *Mountain Biking in the Northern White Mountains,* published by Venture Project, P.O. Box 892, Bethel, ME 04217, (207) 824-3083. This map of rides in the Gorham area was compiled by Mike Micucci, proprietor of Moriah Sports. Also see Berlin quadrangle, USGS 7.5 minute series.

Finding the trail: From Gorham, take NH 16 north. On the edge of town, the road passes underneath a tall steel railroad trestle. Park in the broad parking area under the trestle, on your right.

Source of additional information:

Moriah Sports
101 Main Street
Gorham, NH 03581
(603) 466-5050
Proprietor Mike Micucci is the area's authority on mountain biking.

Notes on the trail: From the parking area, walk your bike across the railroad trestle's pedestrian walkway (watch your head). On the far side, turn right and ride the dirt road to the paper company's dam on the Androscoggin River. Cross the dam by riding between the brick powerhouse and the wooden sheds to the left. Once on the east shore, turn right, onto a dirt road that parallels the river into the woods. Two miles of riding will take you to a junction with a logging road on your left; turn left onto it and follow it up the hill. The trail gets progressively rougher as you climb. After another two miles you cross the Mahoosuc hiking trail (not suitable for mountain biking); about 0.3 mile beyond that, watch for a single-track trail and bear left onto it. It descends through the woods, eventually depositing you on the dirt road along the Androscoggin, upstream of the dam. Turn left, ride back to the dam, and retrace the trail to your starting point.

RIDE 55 · Hayes Copp Ski Trails

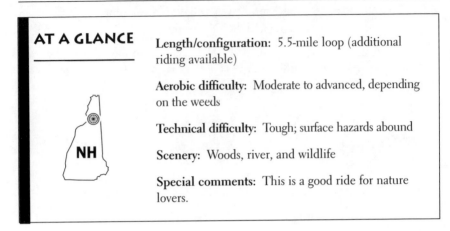

AT A GLANCE

Length/configuration: 5.5-mile loop (additional riding available)

Aerobic difficulty: Moderate to advanced, depending on the weeds

Technical difficulty: Tough; surface hazards abound

Scenery: Woods, river, and wildlife

Special comments: This is a good ride for nature lovers.

If Hayes Copp had given his wife Dolly a mountain bike in 1881, would she have stayed on the farm instead of leaving him for good on their fiftieth wedding anniversary? Probably not—biking on the cross-country ski trails of the former Copp Farm is, to put it kindly, challenging. Boulders, roots, and deadfall trees abound. The bridges can be ridden onto only by the most athletic of bunny-hoppers: decks are a one-foot step above the adjacent trail. Foliage is handlebar-high in places. I walked more than I rode. So why am I glad I did?

Reason One: The last 1.5 miles of this 5.5-mile loop, from the big clearing back to the registration building, were great. Nice, rolling trail, just enough hazards to keep it interesting, and downhill all the way. Those of you who aren't up for technical stuff can do this segment as an out-and-back.

Reason Two: I saw my first moose on a remote segment of this trail: not just one, but a pair of them, parked comfortably in a little depression 30 feet in front of me. I stopped, unsure whether moose are carnivorous predators (I've lived in the city for *way* too long). The female got up and strolled into the woods. Her mate then rose to his feet and took a few steps my way, and we stared at each other for a while. Once assured that his handlebars were indeed larger than mine, he, too, ambled into the woods. A wilderness moment like this can make up for *a lot* of walking.

Reason Three: I found somebody's spare pair of 14-gauge DT spokes (and a broken zip-tie) at a particularly nasty washout. Ten millimeters too long for me, unfortunately. If they're *yours*, and you happened to find my missing camera screws out there, let's make a trade.

General location: 5 miles south of Gorham on NH 16

Elevation change: A few hundred feet of up-and-down, generally in small doses; you'll likely walk much of it for the surface hazards anyhow.

RIDE 55 · Hayes Copp Ski Trails

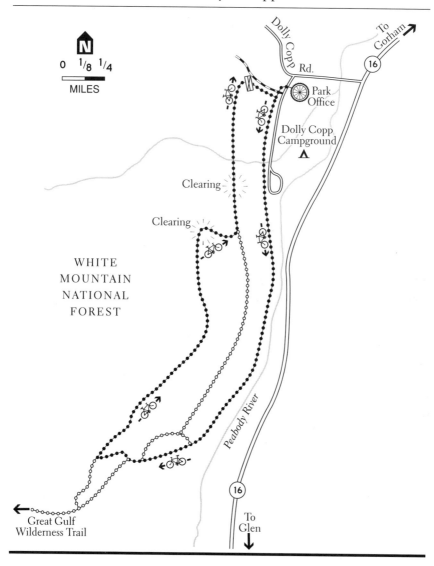

Season: Early summer through fall

Services: You'll find everything you need in Gorham, 5 miles to the north.

Hazards: A veritable smorgasbord of 'em: big boulder patches, big roots, big logs, big brambles, and muddy spots

Rescue index: The trail takes you a couple of miles from civilized areas.

Land status: White Mountain National Forest trails

The trail along the Peabody River abounds with rocks and roots.

Maps: Obtain a ski trail map at the Androscoggin Ranger Station (on NH 16 about 2 miles south of Gorham).

Finding the trail: Park at the campground registration building. If you're doing the loop, pick up the trail past Bathhouse 8 at the End Loop Campsites. If you're just riding up to the clearing and back, look for the trailhead marker at the edge of the parking lot.

Source of additional information:

Androscoggin Ranger Station
White Mountain National Forest
Route 16
Gorham, NH 03581
(603) 466-2713

Notes on the trail: The river trail, marked with blue-diamond blazes, begins at the end loop. It's narrow, wooded, and well stocked with boulders, but is reasonably flat and provides nice views of the Peabody River. Things get muddier as you go, and you'll have to hoist the bike onto the elevated bridge decks that cross some small brooks. Most junctions have signage to help you along.

IMBA says "Don't spook anything with handlebars bigger than yours."

The southern segment of "Rick's Run" marks the approximate halfway point of the loop. It's a steep uphill cutoff, but if you're lucky, you might get to meet a moose or two. Head north on the western trail, which undulates as it follows the hillside. With the weeds, washouts, and fallen trees, it's slow going to the clearing, but the rest of the trip should be a breeze. You'll ride through a second, smaller clearing on the way down. Duck around the gate, hang a sharp right, and return to the parking lot.

RIDE 56 · Moose Brook State Park

AT A GLANCE

NH

Length/configuration: 4-mile loop

Aerobic difficulty: Brace yourself for a big climb.

Technical difficulty: Fun challenges for intermediate cyclists

Scenery: Good overlook of the valley; beaver pond at the top

Special comments: Bring your animal-tracks field guide.

RIDE 56 · Moose Brook State Park

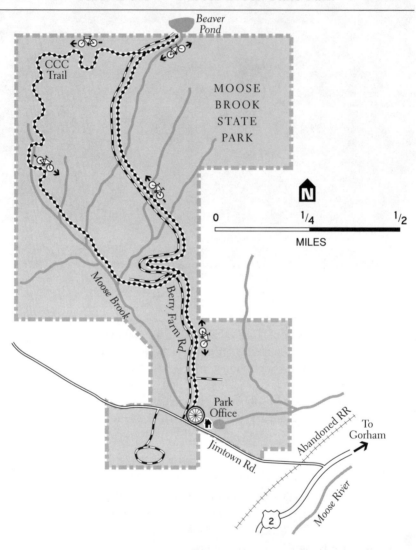

Located just west of Gorham, Moose Brook State Park is the type of facility that every town deserves: a modest-size wooded park with some good mountain biking. This four-mile loop ride heads uphill to the beaver pond on a dirt road, and back on a winding woods path that was carved out by the CCC back in the New Deal era. (Additional CCC trails are being restored by volunteer crews as resources permit.) The path should provide some fun, challenging riding for a cyclist of intermediate skill. A picnic area halfway up to the pond provides a nice view, and

A sign to gladden a
mountain biker's heart.

the farther reaches should afford some good wildlife watching (fresh moose tracks
were evident in several places).

General location: One mile west of Gorham

Elevation change: About 700 feet of climbing to the pond; the return trip on
the path rolls over several smaller hills.

Season: Early summer through fall

Services: Camping is available on-site; other services can be found in Gorham.

Hazards: Watch for muddy spots, rocks, and roots on the woods path.

Rescue index: You'll be within 2 miles of the park office at all times.

Land status: State park

Maps: A trail map is available at the park office.

Finding the trail: From Gorham, take US 2 east and turn right on Jimtown
Road. The park office is ahead on the right and has a small parking area. Check
in with the ranger and pick up a map.

Source of additional information:

Moose Brook State Park
RFD 1
30 Jimtown Road
Gorham, NH 03570
(603) 466-3860

Notes on the trail: From the office, cross the bridge over Perkins Brook and past the group campsites on Berry Farm Road. The ride to the pond gets progressively steeper as you go, but it won't tax your handling skills. About halfway up is a small clearing with a picnic table. Stop, take a drink, and admire the view.

As you reach the top of the climb, several hundred feet before the pond, you'll see the beginning of the CCC Perimeter Path on your left. Turn now, or see the pond first and then return. Here's where the ride gets interesting—work your way past various obstacles, keep your wheels down on the descents, and watch those stream crossings. Keep riding until the trail rejoins Berry Farm Road, bear right, and ride downhill to the starting point. (I didn't see signs for two trails marked on the map that connect with the CCC trail. If you take a turn that I missed, relax. You'll wind up back at the starting point with little if any additional mileage.)

RIDE 57 · Great Glen Trails

AT A GLANCE

NH

Configuration: Cross-country trail network

Aerobic difficulty: Climbing only if you want it

Technical difficulty: Any easier and it'd have to be asphalt.

Scenery: In the shade of Mount Washington

Special comments: It's a good family ride, even for those with training wheels.

"No rocks for me!" you say. "No roots, no washouts, no mud, no unbridged streams, no dense undergrowth, no impossible hills, no cryptic trail maps, no unmarked junctions. I want a trail system that even my five-year-old could ride!" I've got just the place for you: Great Glen Trails, at the foot of the Mount Washington Auto Road. If Walt Disney were around to build a mountain bike park, here's what you'd get.

RIDE 57 · Great Glen Trails

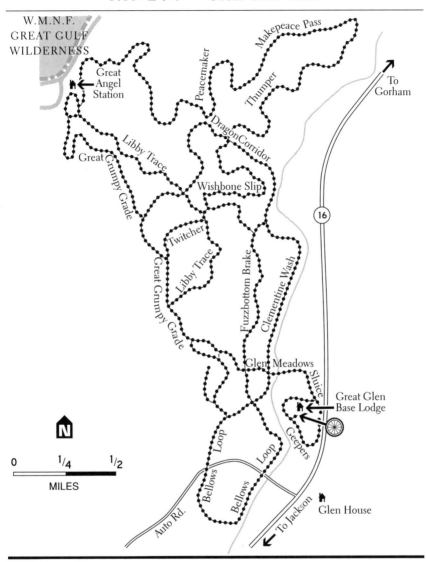

W.M.N.F.
GREAT GULF
WILDERNESS

Great
Angel
Station

Makepeace Pass

To
Gorham

Peacemaker

Thumper

DragonCorridor

Libby Trace

Great Grumpy Grade

Wishbone Slip

16

Twitcher

Libby Trace

Fuzzbottom Brake

Clementine Wash

Great Grumpy Grade

Glen Meadows

Sluice

Great Glen
Base Lodge

N

0   1/4   1/2

MILES

Loop

Bellows Loop

Bellows

Bellows

Geepers

Auto Rd.

To Jackson

Glen House

Of all the cross-country ski facilities I rode, Great Glen has the smoothest trails, built up with a mixture of sand and stone chips and completely purged of surface hazards. Hell, my *driveway* isn't this nice! Great signage and a color-map card help make for real no-brainer riding, and should you need further amusement, trail names like "Cadiddlehopper" and "Fuzzbottom Brake" will keep you snickering. Is it "real" mountain biking? Who cares? (Not me—I'd ridden Hayes Copp the day before.) It's a blast to ride.

General location: 5 miles south of Gorham on NH 16

Elevation change: Lots of small undulations, no killer climbs

Season: Open daily, 8:30 a.m.–5 p.m., Memorial Day weekend through Columbus Day weekend. Rates (in 1997): $5, all day.

Services: Bike rentals and food are available on-site. Other services can be found in Gorham.

Hazards: Hazards? *What* hazards?

Rescue index: You're generally within a mile of the base lodge.

Land status: Privately owned cross-country resort on U.S. Forest Service land

Maps: A full-color trail-map card, and a big fuzzy pipe cleaner to attach the map to your bike, are provided with your trail pass.

Finding the trail: Great Glen Trails is on NH 16, just north of the Mount Washington Auto Road.

Source of additional information:

Great Glen Trails
Pinkham Notch
Box 300
Gorham, NH 03581
(603) 466-2333

UPPER CONNECTICUT
(THE NORTH COUNTRY)

This is the land north of US 2, where rural New Hampshire drops its pretenses and turns its thoughts to matters more mundane than tourism. The factory outlet stores give way to heavy-equipment dealers; the ski condominiums to hunting cabins; gleaming sport-utilities to dusty pickups. Accents become more assuredly Yankee, with a little French Canadian mixed in. Reception of National Weather Service reports, broadcast from downstate, gets spotty. The last of the franchise restaurants lie far to the south — to the north, only a sleepy checkpoint on the Canadian border, and more trees. In the next 70 years, this entire forest will be cut down to provide a lifetime supply of mail-order catalogs — and yet the forest will look exactly the same. This has already happened once, even twice in spots.

In the winter, the area becomes a snowmobiling playground. "Sleds" from all over the northeastern United States fill up village streets and make tracks on the numerous logging roads throughout the woods. As mentioned in the Preface, snowmobiles are big business in New Hampshire, and they're given the run of the place, thanks in large part to the landowner liability coverage paid for by the registration fee.

In the early nineteenth century, when the northern border of the United States was still hazy, the eastern portion of present-day Pittsburg township was the site of a separatist movement known as the Indian Stream Republic. The area's 400 or so residents adopted a constitution in 1832 and spent the next few years attempting to play the governments of New Hampshire, the United States, and Canada against each other. The nobility of their motivations may be judged by their desire to avoid both America's import duties and Canada's draft. Finally, in 1835–36, the New Hampshire state militia marched into Indian Stream to arrest the troublemakers; Canada pledged noninterference; and residents reluctantly accepted New Hampshire rule. The staggering line that separates New Hampshire from Quebec was fixed by the Webster-Ashburton Treaty of 1842.

Mountain biking up here is an adventure in discovery. The trails are here, and plenty of them; it's the accouterments — like maps, shops, and clubs — that are few and far between. The only mountain biking book was published without the consent of the landowner whose territories were described within (at last word, the lawsuit is still pending). Finding the perfect trail calls for persistence and tact in seeking out information from North Country people who love the outdoors but are less eager to sell it than their neighbors to the south.

Suggested Reading: *We Took to the Woods*, by Louise Dickinson Rich. Technically, this is a Maine book—the Rich family lived just over the state line from Errol, on the far side of Umbagog Lake. Her account of making a living in sparsely populated pulpwood country, circa 1940, also describes life in New Hampshire's North Country. Find out the *real* reason why cooks in lumber camps had to lock up their imitation vanilla, learn the many uses of old Model A Ford motors, and don't miss the authentic baked bean recipe.

RIDE 58 · The Balsams

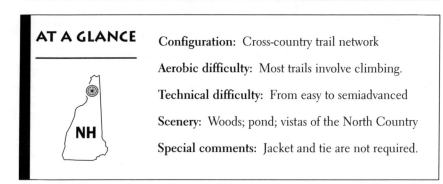

AT A GLANCE

NH

Configuration: Cross-country trail network

Aerobic difficulty: Most trails involve climbing.

Technical difficulty: From easy to semiadvanced

Scenery: Woods; pond; vistas of the North Country

Special comments: Jacket and tie are not required.

Approaching the Balsams Grand Resort Hotel, adjacent to Dixville Notch State Park, is like stepping into a cable rerun of *Runaway with the Rich and Famous*. From its founding in 1866, the Balsams has become one of the premier mountaintop luxury resorts of the Northeast. The place is so huge, so picturesque, so *posh*, you get to wondering if they'll let you drag your muddy old mountain bike near it. Even the highway out front looks as though it were built exclusively for the filming of Lexus commercials.

Well, relax. The Balsams maintains a 30-mile network of bikable trails, and you don't have to rent the Tower Suite to enjoy them. As resort trails go, theirs are pretty rustic—on the outer trails, there are enough surface hazards to challenge a moderately skilled rider. Signage is better than average but might get confusing: trails are designated by a letter (for summer use), a number (for winter), and sometimes a name as well. An excellent full-color map, clearly marked with letter codes keyed to the signs, helps sort it all out. You'll find the Balsams' bike staff quite helpful in recommending a route you'll enjoy, right down to pinpointing recently developed trail hazards. I rode an eight-mile loop that took me

RIDE 58 · The Balsams

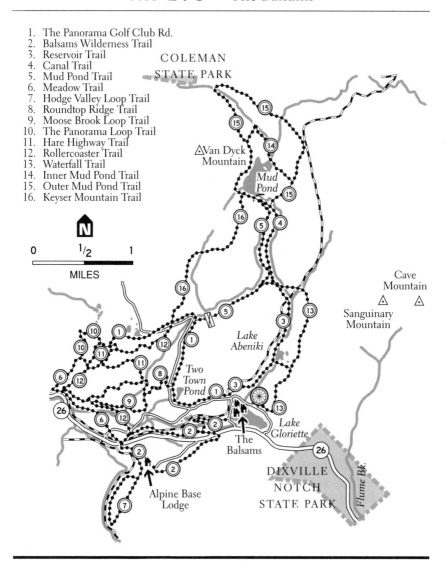

1. The Panorama Golf Club Rd.
2. Balsams Wilderness Trail
3. Reservoir Trail
4. Canal Trail
5. Mud Pond Trail
6. Meadow Trail
7. Hodge Valley Loop Trail
8. Roundtop Ridge Trail
9. Moose Brook Loop Trail
10. The Panorama Loop Trail
11. Hare Highway Trail
12. Rollercoaster Trail
13. Waterfall Trail
14. Inner Mud Pond Trail
15. Outer Mud Pond Trail
16. Keyser Mountain Trail

COLEMAN
STATE PARK

△Van Dyck
Mountain

Mud
Pond

Cave
Mountain

△   △

Sanguinary
Mountain

Lake
Abeniki

Two
Town
Pond

Lake
Gloriette

The
Balsams

DIXVILLE
NOTCH
STATE PARK

Flume Bk.

Alpine Base
Lodge

up to and around Mud Pond, once the resort's source for hydroelectric power (these days, they burn their own wood chips instead).

How can they do all this for such a low trail fee? One stroll around the place, and all the way home you'll be plotting how to make your next million. As soon as I make mine, I'm booking a suite here for our fiftieth wedding anniversary.

General location: Dixville Notch, between Colebrook and Errol on NH 26

It's a long way back to the hotel from here, but why hurry?

Elevation change: There's about a 1,000-foot difference between the lowest and highest points of the system.

Season: Open daily 9 a.m.–4 p.m., mid-May through mid-October. Rates (in 1997): $2; free to guests of the Balsams; discounts at selected motels (ask your innkeeper).

Services: Bike rentals, repairs, dining, and lodging are available on-site. Food and lodging are also available in Colebrook (10 miles west) or Errol (11 miles east).

Hazards: Watch for rocks, roots, waterbars, and occasional mud, especially on the upper trails.

Rescue index: You will be up to 5 miles from the hotel.

Land status: Privately owned resort

Maps: A full-color map with contours is provided with your trail pass.

Finding the trail: The Balsams is just east of the notch. At the lake, take the main road to the hotel. The Mountain Bike and Nature Center, where you'll buy your pass, is across the guest parking area from the hotel proper.

Source of additional information:

The Balsams
Dixville Notch, NH 03576
(603) 255-3400

RIDE 59 · Kelsey Notch

AT A GLANCE

NH

Length/configuration: 21-mile loop

Aerobic difficulty: Long climbs

Technical difficulty: Rough double-track, especially on the west slope

Scenery: Classic North Country wilderness

Special comments: You won't want to leave it to Beavers.

Generally, notches are celebrated bits of New Hampshire geography. Crawford, Franconia, Sandwich, Pinkham, Dixville, and a few others are marked on road maps, extolled in tourist literature, and seen by thousands. Kelsey, on the other hand, is virtually unknown—overshadowed perhaps, by its more dramatic neighbor Dixville. Ride it and you'll have a slice of classic New Hampshire geography pretty much to yourself. The return trip is via NH 26 over Dixville Notch—the climb isn't that bad, and a super-high-speed descent on pavement makes for an exciting finish.

General location: East of Dixville Notch on NH 26

Elevation change: About 1,000 feet of climbing over Kelsey Notch; another 600 feet (on pavement) over Dixville Notch

Season: Early summer through fall

Services: Food and lodging are available in Colebrook (14 miles west) or Errol (7 miles east). Camping is available at Log Haven. Bike repairs, dining, and lodging are available at the Balsams.

Hazards: Watch for surface hazards descending Kelsey Notch, including snowmobile bridges with raised platforms. Watch for traffic while passing through and descending from Dixville Notch.

Rescue index: You will be up to 5 miles from assistance.

Land status: Class VI road, snowmobile trail, and active roads

Maps: Dixville Notch and Blue Mountain quadrangles, USGS 7.5 minute series

Finding the trail: From Dixville Notch, take NH 26 east 4 miles. Kelsey Notch Road is an unmarked dirt road on your right, just after the Millsfield town-line marker and a few hundred feet before Log Haven. Turn onto the road; a few hundred feet beyond you'll find a spot to pull off to the side and park.

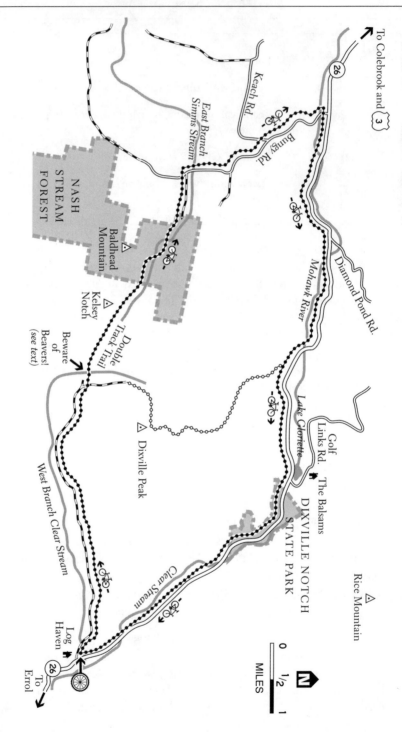

Kinda looks like Santa's very own Christmas tree farm, doesn't it?

Sources of additional information: Copies of the USGS maps for this and other rides are posted for viewing in the Balsams Mountain Bike and Nature Center (just east of Dixville Notch). Trailmaster David Nesbitt can provide details on area mountain biking.

Notes on the trail: From your parking spot, start climbing and keep doing it for the next four miles. There are a few side roads along the way; ignore them—the main road keeps going upward and westward to the notch. Riding is steep at times, but the road is generally in good condition. The first grove of short pines marks an arm of Dixville Peak. You'll descend just a bit before you see a side trail on your right, which leads to Dixville's summit. Continue straight.

Just beyond, the dip in the road is the site of a recurring battle between the Bungy Beavers (a snowmobile club) and the Bungy beavers (a family of furry mammals). When I rode one crisp October afternoon, the mammals were winning: their dam had flooded the road to a depth that almost reached my lower headset races. I carefully scootered through, stopped at the next big rock to drain my shoes, and continued. (A sledder at the Diamond Pond Store vowed that the snowmobilers would have the dam blown before winter.)

A little more climbing brings you to Kelsey Notch, the highest point of the ride, where you'll see another field of little pines. (Kinda looks like Santa's very own Christmas tree farm, doesn't it?) Take your time; catch your breath; enjoy the scenery. Then start down.

The trail is rougher and muddier on the west slope, with an aggressive descent. Watch for waterbars and washouts, keep an eye out for snowmobile trail signage (one section of trail was rerouted recently), and prepare to walk over the bridges. When you've reached the gate, Bungy Road is about three-quarters of a mile ahead.

At Bungy Road, turn right and follow its paved surface down to its junction with NH 26, for about 2.5 miles. Ignore intersecting dirt roads and continue straight past one paved road on the left. The last mile descends sharply: have fun and watch for traffic. At NH 26, turn right. The highway's shoulder is narrow, but traffic is generally light (a truck lane in the last 1.5 miles before the Balsams gives you extra space there). Use extra caution at Dixville Notch; the road crests so sharply that sight distances are very limited. Four miles of high-speed coasting (how does 46 miles per hour on knobbies sound to you?) finishes the ride. Turn onto Kelsey Notch Road again and return to your starting point.

RIDE 60 · Bungy Road

AT A GLANCE	
	Length/configuration: 17-mile loop
	Aerobic difficulty: Repeated climbing
NH	**Technical difficulty:** Easy; graded dirt and asphalt
	Scenery: Rolling farmland of the North Country
	Special comments: This is a good family ride for older children.

Still searching for that perfect mojo for your mountain bike? (A *mojo*, for those who don't know, is an object attached to the bicycle to serve as a good-luck charm, kinda like the figurehead of a wooden sailing ship.) Sure, you've considered Happy Meal toys, rubber alligators, or freeze-dried piranha, but they somehow *lack* something. Why not consider the mojo that's been a favorite with travelers for centuries—a medal of Saint Christopher?

Details are fuzzy, but most versions of Christopher's story portray him as a kind of ferryman who, sometime in the third century, carried the Christ Child on his shoulders across a raging stream. For this, he's become the patron saint of travel-

RIDE 60 · Bungy Road

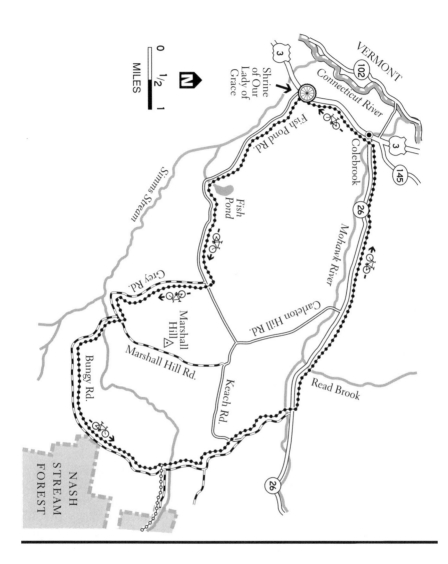

ers, who have dutifully attached Saint Christopher medals to rucksacks, wagons, and automobile sun visors ever since. (Don't hold your breath waiting for the Church to canonize a mountain biking saint—these things take a few centuries.)

Patron saints aren't for everyone, of course, and mountain bikers of evangelical Protestant denominations might be downright uncomfortable with the idea that saints are (to quote the Baltimore Catechism) "the chosen friends of God." On the other hand, doesn't a hasty prayer during a rocky descent make more sense than simply swearing at Shimano?

The best place in the North Country to shop for a Saint Christopher medal also happens to be the starting point for this ride: the Shrine of Our Lady of Grace, just south of Colebrook. Spread over several acres, the shrine features religious sculpture in granite and Carrara marble, a "living rosary" (spectacularly lit at night), and an outdoor way of the cross. It's an impressive monument to faith, and a good place for contemplation.

General location: Colebrook

Elevation change: About 1,000 feet, mostly in the first half of the ride

Season: Early June through fall

Services: Lodging, camping, and food can be found in the Colebrook area. The nearest place for bike repairs is the Balsams (see Ride 58), on NH 26 at Dixville Notch.

Hazards: Watch for moderate traffic on NH 26, on US 3, and in Colebrook.

Rescue index: You are on public roads throughout the ride; inhabited areas are never more than a mile away.

Land status: Graded dirt roads and paved public roads

Maps: Page 50 of DeLorme's *New Hampshire Atlas and Gazetteer.* Also see Blue Mountain quadrangle, USGS 7.5 minute series.

Finding the trail: The shrine is a mile south of Colebrook on US 3. Ample parking is available there (admission is free, though donations are appreciated).

Source of additional information:

Shrine of Our Lady of Grace
Route 3
Colebrook, NH 03576
(603) 237-5511

Notes on the trail: From the shrine, take Fish Pond Road east and up the hill (the intersection with US 3 is adjacent to the grounds and across the street from where you parked). The road, which is paved, climbs for several hundred feet, then levels off and twists through woods dotted with houses. After about 3.5 miles, an unmarked dirt road appears on the right. This is Grey Road; turn onto it. A long downgrade takes you to a sharp left bend; about 0.4 mile after the bend, turn right onto Bungy Road (which is also dirt).

Bungy Road cuts a lazy arc against the base of the mountains, connecting with several logging roads along the way. Stay on the main road. For several miles, it's narrow and wooded, dotted with the occasional hunting cabin. Then it opens up and asphalt appears, and so do farmhouses. The last 1.5 miles of Bungy Road are a screamin' paved descent; ignore the one paved road you'll see on the left, and keep an eye out for the occasional car. Bungy Road ends at NH 26; turn left and ride about 4.5 miles into the village of Colebrook. (On the outskirts of town you'll see a heavy-equipment dealer whose varied inventory is parked for several hundred feet along both sides of the road.) At Colebrook, turn left on US 3 to return to the shrine.

RIDE 61 · Stewartstown Hollow

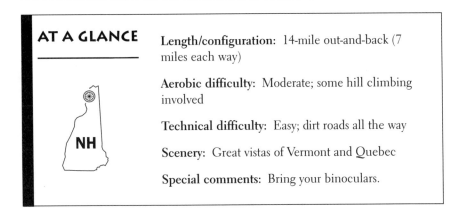

AT A GLANCE

Length/configuration: 14-mile out-and-back (7 miles each way)

Aerobic difficulty: Moderate; some hill climbing involved

Technical difficulty: Easy; dirt roads all the way

Scenery: Great vistas of Vermont and Quebec

Special comments: Bring your binoculars.

Some of the rides I've described in this book take you into the wilderness. Some take you into the past. This one simply takes you into the country. From end to end, you're surrounded by *ruralness*. The paper mill lies just over the hill in West Stewartstown, and logging operations go on in small plots all around. Besides that, not much happens around here, and that's just fine.

The ruralness is reflected in the houses you'll see along the way. Nobody's trying to catch the eye of a passing tourist. No one's keeping up with the Joneses. No one has fashioned their domicile into a New England picture-postcard fantasy. They're just houses in the country. It reminds me of where I grew up, actually. (I'll bet the first day of deer season is a school holiday here, too.)

This ride follows public roads all the way, so forget about technique for a while and absorb the surroundings.

General location: Stewartstown Hollow, about 5 miles north of Colebrook on NH 145

Elevation change: About 1,100 feet, riding the dirt roads in both directions (you save about 300 feet climbing if you return via NH 145)

Season: Late spring through fall

Services: Food, lodging, and camping can be found in Colebrook, or in Pittsburg, 5 miles north on NH 145. The nearest place for bike repairs is at the Balsams (see Ride 58).

Hazards: Watch for the occasional pickup truck.

RIDE 61 · Stewartstown Hollow

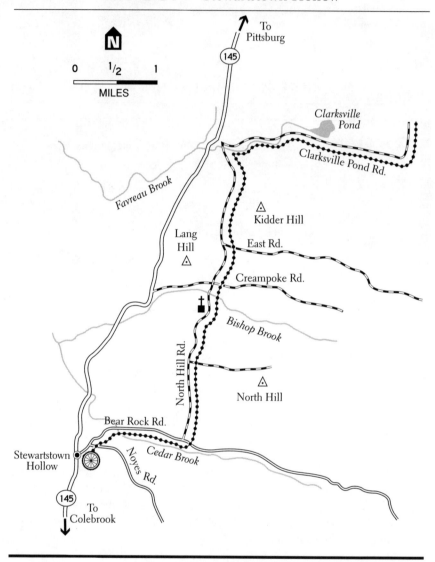

Rescue index: The entire ride passes through lightly inhabited areas.

Land status: Public roads

Maps: Page 52 of DeLorme's *New Hampshire Atlas and Gazetteer*. Also see Lovering Mountain and Pittsburg quadrangles, USGS 7.5 minute series.

Finding the trail: From Colebrook, take NH 145 north about 5 miles. Stewartstown Hollow is a small settlement at the intersection with Bear Rock

North Hill Cemetery, along a quiet country road in Stewartstown Hollow.

Road. Turn right onto Bear Rock Road; you'll see a wide spot along the shoulder for parking.

Source of additional information:

North Country Chamber of Commerce
Box 1
Colebrook, NH 03576

Notes on the trail: From Stewartstown Hollow, take Bear Rock Road for about 1.4 miles (it climbs most of the way). To your left, you'll see a dirt road that climbs steeply. This is North Hill Road; turn left. As you gain altitude, the road narrows; you'll ride through a "tunnel" of pines before some excellent views appear on your left. A descent takes you past the North Hill Cemetery, across an intersecting dirt road, and up another hill (with another scenic overlook).

At the bottom of this second hill, the road ends at the paved highway, NH 145. Just a few hundred feet *before* that, turn sharply right onto a dirt road that takes you uphill once more. You're on the final leg, up to Clarksville Pond. By the way, you're also on the 45th Parallel, which means that you're halfway between the equator and the North Pole. (Don't forget to tell your friends when you get home.)

The pond, with cottages and woods around it, will be visible on your left as you continue for another mile or so beyond. When the road ends at a private driveway, turn around and head back. (You can take a shortcut, if you so choose, by turning left onto NH 145.)

RIDE 62 · Lake Francis

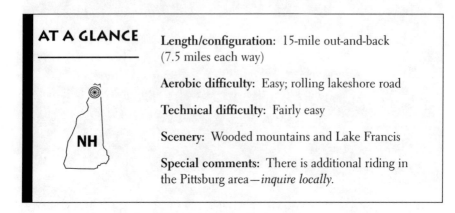

AT A GLANCE

Length/configuration: 15-mile out-and-back (7.5 miles each way)

Aerobic difficulty: Easy; rolling lakeshore road

Technical difficulty: Fairly easy

Scenery: Wooded mountains and Lake Francis

Special comments: There is additional riding in the Pittsburg area—*inquire locally.*

Among off-road bicyclists in the Granite State, none has achieved more notoriety than Mountain Bike Steve. He lives downstate, and for years, he has taken off from the flatlands on weekends to ride the trails and logging roads of the North Country. Steve approaches mountain biking as a character-building wilderness experience, a kind of "Iron John on Knobbies," if you will. He hits the trail with little more than a one-speed mountain bike, a water bottle, and some Good-and-Plenty candy. He advocates a strict training regimen. He's ridden to the farthest reaches of just about every trail in the North Country. A few years ago, he wrote a book that details his mountain biking philosophies and tips, and maps out a number of rides in the wilderness. Good book, but with one problem: it blew the lid off the only significant trail-access controversy in all of New Hampshire.

Most of the rides Steve described are on land belonging to the Champion International Corporation. The company was not pleased to see its lands advertised as a mountain biking mecca. In the past, company personnel had usually turned a blind eye toward mountain bikers, so long as they weren't near an area being actively logged. With Steve's book, the official company line became "no bikes." Company managers had visions of roads crowded with bikes (they're already crowded with snowmobiles in winter) and all the grief that would ensue if one mountain biker met with disaster on their property. A total ban seemed the only sensible way out of a potential liability nightmare. They *do* have trees to cut, after all. Mountain Bike Steve found himself the poster boy for Everything That's Wrong with Mountain Bikers, a role none of us would enjoy much.

These days, the furor has died down, and Champion's policy has softened somewhat. Mountain bikers are quietly being allowed into some inactive areas, but you'll have to ask around once you get to Pittsburg. The North Country Chamber of Commerce can point you toward trails where mountain biking is permitted.

RIDE 62 · Lake Francis

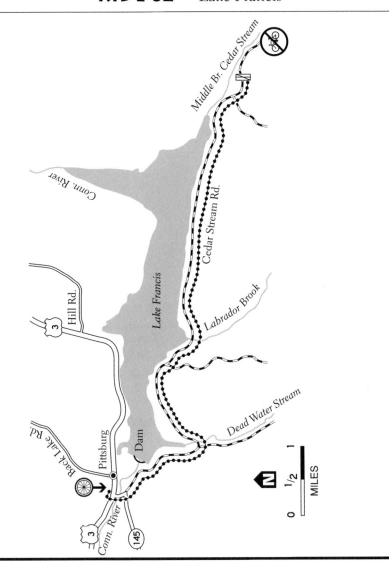

The ride described here follows a public road, so access isn't a problem. You'll follow the south shore of Lake Francis, a large reservoir just downstream of the Connecticut Lakes chain.

General location: Pittsburg

Elevation change: The road follows a few undulations along the lakeshore but is more or less level.

Season: Early summer to mid-October

Services: Food and lodging can be found in and around Pittsburg. The nearest place for bike repairs is at the Balsams (see Ride 58).

Hazards: Watch for occasional traffic.

Rescue index: You may or may not be able to find help along the way, depending on the season. The dwellings along the route are vacation cottages.

Land status: Town road

Maps: This and other trails are marked on a sheet map of the Pittsburg area, produced by Liebl Printing and sold by Pittsburg retailers.

Finding the trail: The ride starts in Pittsburg; park along US 3 in the village.

Source of additional information:

> North Country Chamber of Commerce
> Box 1
> Colebrook, NH 03576
> At this writing, mountain bike inquiries were being handled by Chamber of Commerce member Paul Bergeron, proprietor of Ramblewood Cabins and Campground in Pittsburg. He can be reached at (603) 538-6948.

Notes on the trail: From Pittsburg, take NH 145 south for a few hundred feet—just long enough to cross the river. Take a left turn onto Cedar Stream Road, which is dirt. Before long, you'll see Murphy Dam on your left and the lake behind it. Cedar Stream Road loosely follows the lakeshore; ignore all side roads you'll pass on the right. (For those curious to explore the side roads, I've been told that the "No Wheeled Vehicles" signs posted by the Department of Fish and Game are intended to keep out motorcycles and ATVs, *not* mountain bikes.)

After about seven miles, you reach the far end of the lake, but the road continues. Keep riding until you reach the gate, which marks the beginning of the private logging road. (The logging road continues for another 17 miles over hills, and it ends at US 3 just above First Connecticut Lake. Be on your best behavior; someday you might be allowed to ride this.) At the gate, turn around and return to Pittsburg.

AFTERWORD

A few years ago I wrote a long piece on this issue for *Sierra* magazine that entailed calling literally dozens of government land managers, game wardens, mountain bikers, and local officials to get a feeling for how riders were being welcomed on the trails. All that I've seen personally since, and heard from my authors, indicates there hasn't been much change. We're still considered the new kid on the block. We have less of a right to the trails than horses and hikers, and we're excluded from many areas, including:

a) wilderness areas

b) national parks (except on roads, and those paths specifically marked "bike path")

c) national monuments (except on roads open to the public)

d) most state parks and monuments (except on roads, and those paths specifically marked "bike path")

e) an increasing number of urban and county parks, especially in California (except on roads, and those paths specifically marked "bike path")

Frankly, I have little difficulty with these exclusions and would, in fact, restrict our presence from some trails I've ridden (one time) due to the environmental damage and chance of blind-siding the many walkers and hikers I met up with along the way. But these are my personal views. The author of this volume and mountain bikers as a group may hold different opinions.

You can do your part in keeping us from being excluded from even more trails by riding responsibly. Many local and national off-road bicycle organizations have been formed with exactly this in mind, and one of the largest—the National Off-Road Bicycle Association (NORBA)—offers the following code of behavior for mountain bikers:

1. I will yield the right of way to other non-motorized recreationists. I realize that people judge all cyclists by my actions.

2. I will slow down and use caution when approaching or overtaking another cyclist and will make my presence known well in advance.

3. I will maintain control of my speed at all times and will approach turns in anticipation of someone around the bend.

4. I will stay on designated trails to avoid trampling native vegetation and minimize potential erosion to trails by not using muddy trails or short-cutting switchbacks.

5. I will not disturb wildlife or livestock.

6. I will not litter. I will pack out what I pack in, and pack out more than my share whenever possible.

7. I will respect public and private property, including trail use signs and no trespassing signs, and I will leave gates as I have found them.

8. I will always be self-sufficient and my destination and travel speed will be determined by my ability, my equipment, the terrain, the present and potential weather conditions.

9. I will not travel solo when bikepacking in remote areas. I will leave word of my destination and when I plan to return.

10. I will observe the practice of minimum impact bicycling by "taking only pictures and memories and leaving only waffle prints."
11. I will always wear a helmet whenever I ride.

Now, I have a problem with some of these—number nine, for instance. The most enjoyable mountain biking I've ever done has been solo. And as for leaving word of destination and time of return, I've enjoyed living in such a way as to say, "I'm off to pedal Colorado. See you in the fall." Of course it's senseless to take needless risks, and I plan a ride and pack my gear with this in mind. But for me number nine smacks too much of the "never-out-of-touch" mentality. And getting away from civilization, deep into the wilds, is, for many people, what mountain biking's all about.

All in all, however, NORBA's is a good list, and surely we mountain bikers would be liked more, and excluded less, if we followed the suggestions. But let me offer a "code of ethics" I much prefer, one given to cyclists by Utah's Wasatch-Cache National Forest office.

Study a Forest Map Before You Ride
Currently, bicycles are permitted on roads and developed trails within the Wasatch-Cache National Forest except in designated Wilderness. If your route crosses private land, it is your responsibility to obtain right of way permission from the landowner.

Keep Groups Small
Riding in large groups degrades the outdoor experience for others, can disturb wildlife, and usually leads to greater resource damage.

Avoid Riding on Wet Trails
Bicycle tires leave ruts in wet trails. These ruts concentrate runoff and accelerate erosion. Postponing a ride when the trails are wet will preserve the trails for future use.

Stay on Roads and Trails
Riding cross-country destroys vegetation and damages the soil.

Always Yield to Others
Trails are shared by hikers, horses, and bicycles. Move off the trail to allow horses to pass and stop to allow hikers adequate room to share the trail. Simply yelling "Bicycle!" is not acceptable.

Control Your Speed
Excessive speed endangers yourself and other forest users.

Avoid Wheel Lock-up and Spin-out
Steep terrain is especially vulnerable to trail wear. Locking brakes on steep descents or when stopping needlessly damages trails. If a slope is steep enough to require locking wheels and skidding, dismount and walk your bicycle. Likewise, if an ascent is so steep your rear wheel slips and spins, dismount and walk your bicycle.

Protect Waterbars and Switchbacks
Waterbars, the rock and log drains built to direct water off trails, protect trails from erosion. When you encounter a waterbar, ride directly over the top or dismount and walk your bicycle. Riding around the ends of waterbars destroys them and speeds erosion. Skidding around switchback corners shortens trail life. Slow down for switchback corners and keep your wheels rolling.

If You Abuse It, You Lose It
Mountain bikers are relative newcomers to the forest and must prove themselves responsible trail users. By following the guidelines above, and by participating in trail maintenance service projects, bicyclists can help avoid closures which would prevent them from using trails.

I've never seen a better trail-etiquette list for mountain bikers. So have fun. Be careful. And don't screw up things for the next rider.

Dennis Coello
Series Editor

GLOSSARY

This short list of terms does not contain all the words used by mountain bike enthusiasts when discussing their sport. But it should serve as an introduction to the lingo you'll hear on the trails.

ATB   all-terrain bike; this, like "fat-tire bike," is another name for a mountain bike

ATV   all-terrain vehicle; this usually refers to the loud, fume-spewing three- or four-wheeled motorized vehicles you will not enjoy meeting on the trail—except, of course, if you crash and have to hitch a ride out on one

bladed   refers to a dirt road which has been smoothed out by the use of a wide blade on earth-moving equipment; "blading" gets rid of the teeth-chattering, much-cursed washboards found on so many dirt roads after heavy vehicle use

blaze   a mark on a tree made by chipping away a piece of the bark, usually done to designate a trail; such trails are sometimes described as "blazed"

blind corner a curve in the road or trail that conceals bikers, hikers, equestrians, and other traffic

BLM   Bureau of Land Management, an agency of the federal government

buffed   used to describe a very smooth trail

catching air taking a jump in such a way that both wheels of the bike are off the ground at the same time

clean	while this may describe what you and your bike won't be after following many trails, the term is most often used as a verb to denote the action of pedaling a tough section of trail successfully
combination	this type of route may combine two or more configurations; for example, a point-to-point route may integrate a scenic loop or an out-and-back spur midway through the ride; likewise, an out-and-back may have a loop at its farthest point (this configuration looks like a cherry with a stem attached; the stem is the out-and-back, the fruit is the terminus loop); or a loop route may have multiple out-and-back spurs and/or loops to the side; mileage for a combination route is for the total distance to complete the ride
dab	touching the ground with a foot or hand
deadfall	a tangled mass of fallen trees or branches
diversion	ditch a usually narrow, shallow ditch dug across or around a trail; funneling the water in this manner keeps it from destroying the trail
double-track	the dual tracks made by a jeep or other vehicle, with grass or weeds or rocks between; mountain bikers can ride in either of the tracks, but you will of course find that whichever one you choose, and no matter how many times you change back and forth, the other track will appear to offer smoother travel
dugway	a steep, unpaved, switchbacked descent
endo	flipping end over end
feathering	using a light touch on the brake lever, hitting it lightly many times rather than very hard or locking the brake
four-wheel-drive	this refers to any vehicle with drive-wheel capability on all four wheels (a jeep, for instance, has four-wheel drive as compared with a two-wheel-drive passenger car), or to a rough road or trail that requires four-wheel-drive capability (or a one-wheel-drive mountain bike!) to negotiate it
game trail	the usually narrow trail made by deer, elk, or other game
gated	everyone knows what a gate is, and how many variations exist upon this theme; well, if a trail is described as "gated" it simply has a gate across it; don't forget that the rule is if you find a gate closed, close it behind you; if you find one open, leave it that way

Giardia	shorthand for Giardia lamblia, and known as the "backpacker's bane" until we mountain bikers expropriated it; this is a waterborne parasite that begins its life cycle when swallowed, and one to four weeks later has its host (you) bloated, vomiting, shivering with chills and living in the bathroom; the disease can be avoided by "treating" (purifying) the water you acquire along the trail (see "Hitting the Trail" in the Introduction)
gnarly	a term thankfully used less and less these days, it refers to tough trails
hammer	to ride very hard
hardpack	a trail in which the dirt surface is packed down hard; such trails make for good and fast riding, and very painful landings; bikers most often use "hardpack" as both a noun and adjective, and "hard-packed" as an adjective only (the grammar lesson will help you when diagramming sentences in camp)
hike-a-bike	what you do when the road or trail becomes too steep or rough to remain in the saddle
jeep road, jeep trail	a rough road or trail passable only with four-wheel-drive capability (or a horse or mountain bike)
kamikaze	while this once referred primarily to those Japanese fliers who quaffed a glass of sake, then flew off as human bombs in suicide missions against U.S. naval vessels, it has more recently been applied to the idiot mountain bikers who, far less honorably, scream down hiking trails, endangering the physical and mental safety of the walking, biking, and equestrian traffic they meet; deck guns were necessary to stop the Japanese kamikaze pilots, but a bike pump or walking staff in the spokes is sufficient for the current-day kamikazes who threaten to get us all kicked off the trails
loop	this route configuration is characterized by riding from the designated trailhead to a distant point, then returning to the trailhead via a different route (or simply continuing on the same in a circle route) without doubling back; you always move forward across new terrain, but return to the starting point when finished; mileage is for the entire loop from the trailhead back to trailhead
multi-purpose	a BLM designation of land which is open to many uses; mountain biking is allowed

ORV	a motorized off-road vehicle
out-and-back	a ride where you will return on the same trail you pedaled out; while this might sound far more boring than a loop route, many trails look very different when pedaled in the opposite direction
pack stock	horses, mules, llamas, et cetera, carrying provisions along the trails . . . and unfortunately leaving a trail of their own behind
point-to-point	a vehicle shuttle (or similar assistance) is required for this type of route, which is ridden from the designated trailhead to a distant location, or endpoint, where the route ends; total mileage is for the one-way trip from the trailhead to endpoint
portage	to carry your bike on your person
pummy	volcanic activity in the Pacific Northwest and elsewhere produces soil with a high content of pumice; trails through such soil often become thick with dust, but this is light in consistency and can usually be pedaled; remember, however, to pedal carefully, for this dust obscures whatever might lurk below
quads	bikers use this term to refer both to the extensor muscle in the front of the thigh (which is separated into four parts) and to USGS maps; the expression "Nice quads!" refers always to the former, however, except in those instances when the speaker is an engineer
runoff	rainwater or snowmelt
scree	an accumulation of loose stones or rocky debris lying on a slope or at the base of a hill or cliff
signed	a "signed" trail has signs in place of blazes
single-track	a single, narrow path through grass or brush or over rocky terrain, often created by deer, elk, or backpackers; single-track riding is some of the best fun around
slickrock	the rock-hard, compacted sandstone that is great to ride and even prettier to look at; you'll appreciate it even more if you think of it as a petrified sand dune or seabed (which it is), and if the rider before you hasn't left tire marks (from unnecessary skidding) or granola bar wrappers behind
snowmelt	runoff produced by the melting of snow
snowpack	unmelted snow accumulated over weeks or months of winter—or over years in high-mountain terrain

spur	a road or trail that intersects the main trail you're following
switchback	a zigzagging road or trail designed to assist in traversing steep terrain: mountain bikers should not skid through switchbacks
technical	terrain that is difficult to ride due not to its grade (steepness) but to its obstacles—rocks, roots, logs, ledges, loose soil. . .
topo	short for topographical map, the kind that shows both linear distance and elevation gain and loss; "topo" is pronounced with both vowels long
trashed	a trail that has been destroyed (same term used no matter what has destroyed it . . . cattle, horses, or even mountain bikers riding when the ground was too wet)
two-wheel-drive	this refers to any vehicle with drive-wheel capability on only two wheels (a passenger car, for instance, has two-wheel-drive); a two-wheel-drive road is a road or trail easily traveled by an ordinary car
waterbar	An earth, rock, or wooden structure that funnels water off trails to reduce erosion
washboarded	a road that is surfaced with many ridges spaced closely together, like the ripples on a washboard; these make for very rough riding, and even worse driving in a car or jeep
whoop-de-doo	closely spaced dips or undulations in a trail; these are often encountered in areas traveled heavily by ORVs
wilderness area	land that is officially set aside by the federal government to remain natural—pure, pristine, and untrammeled by any vehicle, including mountain bikes; though mountain bikes had not been born in 1964 (when the United States Congress passed the Wilderness Act, establishing the National Wilderness Preservation system), they are considered a "form of mechanical transport" and are thereby excluded; in short, stay out
wind chill	a reference to the wind's cooling effect upon exposed flesh; for example, if the temperature is 10 degrees Fahrenheit and the wind is blowing at 20 miles per hour, the wind-chill (that is, the actual temperature to which your skin reacts) is minus 32 degrees; if you are riding in wet conditions things are even worse, for the wind-chill would then be minus 74 degrees!
windfall	anything (trees, limbs, brush, fellow bikers . . .) blown down by the wind

INDEX

ABOUT THE AUTHOR

JEFF FAUST first repacked a Bendix coaster-brake hub at the age of 13, and ever since, bicycles have been an important part of his life. Besides such activities as winter commuting, bike-club newsletter editing, and inn-to-inn tour leading, he's had some truly unique cycling experiences as well: drafting a moving

diesel locomotive ("It was just a yard switcher going 10 mph," he says) and riding through the abandoned tunnels of the Pennsylvania Turnpike ("What a bore," he says of the ride. "Well, two, actually."). When not immersed in the world of travel writing, Jeff works in the print shop at a toy factory. He lives with his wife and young son in Rochester, New York, where he enjoys collecting toy trains, repairing antique kitchen appliances, and brewing beer. This is his third book. He is currently at work on an illustrated history of the interstate highway system.

"Live Free or Die" is not only New Hampshi___ reflection of the state's attitude toward mountain biking. The combination of liberal mountain biking policies and some of the most beautiful scenery in the free world is a fortuitous one for off-road enthusiasts. *Mountain Bike! New Hampshire* will introduce you to the thrill of exploring some of the northeast's most beautiful mountains, forests, and lakes while you experience the state's most unforgettable rides.

Mountain Bike! New Hampshire provides detailed information on over 60 classic rides, including tours through the White Mountains and the Lakes Region. Author Jeff Faust has selected a diverse collection of trails that offer something for novice and expert mountain bikers alike. From a technical ride among towering peaks to a mellow jaunt along a wooded, paved path, if it's good riding, it's profiled here.

Each route profile features:
- at-a-glance key information
- a thorough ride description
- a detailed trail map
- helpful sources of information
- proximity of important services
- valuable commentary on elevation changes and possible hazards
- a rescue index

Mountain Bike! New Hampshire also features entertaining photographs, vivid descriptions of native flora and fauna, a glossary of mountain biking terms, and tips on mountain biking etiquette. And that's not all—Faust shares fascinating historical facts and regional anecdotes about the most fat-tire friendly state in the Union.

Jeff Faust, a lifelong cyclist, lives in Rochester, New York. He is also the author of *Rochester by Bike* and has led inn-to-inn bicycle tours and edited bike club newsletters. *Mountain Bike! New Hampshire* is one of many great titles in editor Dennis Coello's *America by Mountain Bike* series. Other titles include *Mountain Bike! Vermont* and *Mountain Bike! Maine*.

MENASHA RIDGE PRESS
BIRMINGHAM, ALABAMA

Distributed by
**The Globe
Pequot Press**

ISBN 0-89732-268-1

51595>

EAN

9 780897 322683

ISBN 0-89732-268-1

00268>

UPC

6 12106 01595 8

MOUNTAIN BIKING—TRAVEL   US $15.95